Guide
to
Teaching Percussion

Guide
to
Teaching Percussion

by

Harry R. Bartlett

Second Edition

by

Ronald A. Holloway
Sacramento State College

WM. C. BROWN COMPANY PUBLISHERS
Dubuque, Iowa

MUSIC SERIES

Consulting Editor
Frederick W. Westphal
Sacramento State College

Copyright © 1964 by Harry R. Bartlett

Copyright © 1971 by Wm. C. Brown Company Publishers

Library of Congress Catalog Card Number: 70—157815

ISBN 0—697—03492—5

Printed in the United States of America

Preface

Mr. Bartlett, in preparing the original edition of the *Guide To Teaching Percussion*, created an extremely thorough and accurate percussion reference book. The *Guide* has served and will continue to serve well the purpose for which it was primarily developed—the pre-service and in-service training of instrumental music teachers.

In this second edition the entire text has been reviewed. In some areas it has been reworded, in others expanded, and in still others it has been revised completely. New figures and illustrations have been added. Newer techniques of performance have been introduced throughout. The chapter on Marching Band Percussion has been enlarged. The Annotated Bibliography has been reorganized and expanded.

Throughout this revision a concerted effort has been made to avoid the pitfalls of controversy arising primarily from differences in pedagogical philosophy. When newer or different techniques have been introduced, they have been done so with the knowledge that they are accepted by the majority of today's percussionists and are not just the whims of one instructor or performer.

I would like to express my sincere appreciation to Mr. Leonard Cramer of Sacramento State College for his assistance in producing all new photographs utilized in this second edition.

Ronald A. Holloway

Preface to
First Edition

My aim in producing the *Guide to Teaching Percussion* has been to gather and organize as much practical and theoretical material as possible concerning percussion instruments, their playing techniques and teaching procedures. To this end I have drawn both from my own experience as a player and teacher of the percussion instruments and from the published and unpublished writings and experiences of other teacher-musicians. The need for such a comprehensive reference source is attested to by the fact that to date no such work has appeared in print. When one considers the enormity of the world of percussion—some fifty-six instruments are treated in this book—it is an admittedly presumptuous undertaking to attempt a thorough treatment of every facet of the subject. I should like to assure the reader, however, that I have assumed this risk not out of presumptuousness but because of my belief that such a work may fill a genuine need.

The *Guide* is organized in ten chapters and an appendix, with each topic listed separately in the Table of Contents for easy reference. Chapter 1 contains introductory material which serves as orientation to the basic concepts of percussion playing and the author's pedagogical viewpoint. Chapter 2 consists of a comprehensive chart of 56 percussion instruments showing their physical and acoustical properties, methods of playing, and characteristic usages. Chapters 3 through 8 deal with the snare drum, bass drum and cymbals, mallet-played instruments, timpani, other percussion instruments, and Latin-American instruments, respectively. Dance band drumming is the subject of Chapter 9, and Chapter 10 treats the percussion section of the marching band. The Appendix contains varied material of a less technical, yet very useful, nature. Included are such topics as *Stage Deportment for the Percussion Section,* an *Annotated Bibliography of Percussion Teaching Materials,* and a *Glossary of Percussion Terms.*

The procedure in each of the chapters has been to begin with pertinent historical data, introduce the basic playing techniques, and conclude with teaching procedures and suggestions. To help the reader develop clear and accurate concepts of the various physical actions used to produce the tones of the percussion instruments, liberal use has been made throughout of photographs and diagrams. Many of these photographs are arranged to show the stepwise progress of a single action, in the manner of movie "stills."

The philosophy underlying the *Guide* might be summarized as follows: 1) percussion technique should be developed to serve *musical* ends; 2) recommended techniques and styles should be those most generally used by artist-percussionists currently active in music performance; 3) though the snare drum may rightly be considered the basic percussion instrument, the ability to execute the "original 26 rudiments" does not make a percussionist; 4) demonstration-imitation is the best method for teaching skills such as those neuromuscular coordinations used in manipulating sticks, mallets and beaters; 5) percussion teaching should inculcate a feeling of pride on the part of the student in performing every assignment, no matter how small, with care and musical feeling.

The *Guide* has been developed primarily as a reference book for use in the pre-service and in-service training of instrumental music teachers. It could also serve as a basic textbook in the usual instrumental methods classes at the college level. Teachers in the field should find the *Guide* a source of new ideas and a ready reference for solution of the innumerable problems which come up in connection with the interpretation and performance of percussion parts. In similar ways the *Guide* should prove of value to the studio instructor teaching privately. The needs of advanced percussion students, professional percussionists, and conductors, composers and arrangers of music have been kept in mind, too. For these readers the descriptive information on the standard and more esoteric percussion instruments, their typical idiomatic usages and playing techniques, and the glossary of terms in four languages should prove worthwhile.

I wish to express my heartfelt gratitude to the following organizations and individuals for their assistance in the preparation of this book: the Ludwig Drum Co., the G. C. Jenkins Co., the A. Zildjian Co., and the Norren Co. for furnishing photographs of their products for inclusion in the text; the Leeds Music Corp. for permission to reproduce the percussion parts of *Legend* by Paul Creston; musician-photographer Weldon Pollard of Oakland, California, for his skill and patience in working with me on the many photographs required to illustrate the concepts involved in percussion technique; my father, Richard F. Bartlett, for the drawings and diagrams; Jere O'Boyle of Musicopy, San Francisco, for the music autographing; and to my wife, Betty Bartlett, for her inspiration, encouragement, and many, many hours of work in the preparation of the manuscript.

Harry R. Bartlett

Contents

CHAPTER 1

Introduction

BASIC CONCEPTS OF PERCUSSION PLAYING

Tone Production

The sound-producing vibration of any percussion instrument is made by a quick, resilient blow. The drumstick, beater, or mallet must "get-on-and-get-off" the vibrating drumhead, bar, or plate. Any lingering of the beater on the surface tends to stop the vibration. See Figure 1.1. Percussion instruments must be struck (played) in such a way that the tone is drawn out of the instrument rather than pounded into it.

Three factors influence the tone quality of percussion instruments: (1) the physical properties of the instruments themselves: resonance of the materials, adjustments of the heads and snares, choice of sticks, beaters, or mallets; (2) the place at which the surface is struck; and, (3) the manner in which the surface is struck.

To achieve good quality of tone from percussion instruments, it is imperative that the vibration be free and not interfered with by stiff, lingering blows.

Attack and Release of Tones

The character of the percussion instruments demands that the start of a tone be accented slightly. The attack, even at *pp* volume, should be crisp, definite and fall precisely on the beat. Snare drum rolls, for example, require a slight accenting of the initial blow to set the drumhead into vibration, thus starting the tone at precisely the right instant. The larger the instrument, the slower it "speaks." The bass drum, large tam-tams (gongs), large cymbals, and

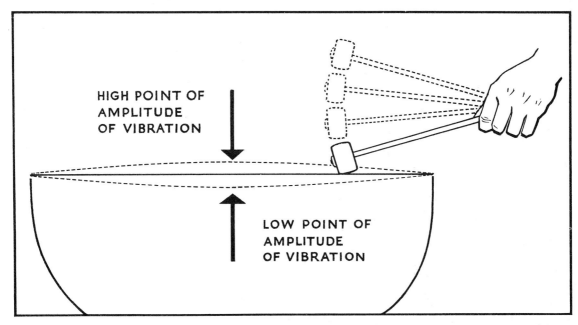

HIGH POINT OF
AMPLITUDE
OF VIBRATION

LOW POINT OF
AMPLITUDE
OF VIBRATION

Figure 1.1. Vibration of drumhead.

timpani thus require great care in timing by the player.

The stopping (release) of the tone is done by pressing or grasping the vibrating surface with the finger tips or hands. Damping is the term used in percussion playing to refer to the stopping or release of tone.

The following are important applications of the concept of damping:

1. Allow the tone to ring for the written duration of the note, then damp it. (Exceptions are noted in succeeding chapters.)
2. Damping should be instantaneous and complete.
3. Drumheads not being played upon will ring sympathetically, so there must also be damping of these heads at such places in the music as general pauses, cut-offs at ends of fermatas, and final notes.
4. The snare drum requires damping in many passages. Even though the snare drum has only a short after-ring, no sound should spill over into a general silence.
5. The tone must be allowed to project before being damped, even on notes marked *staccato*, *sfz*, or *secco* (dry, short).
6. A tie or slur mark after a triangle, cymbal, bass drum, chime, bell, or timpani note means to let the tone ring considerably longer than the written value of the note. For example:

Dynamic Contrasts

Musical percussion playing demands careful attention to the dynamic level at all times. Second in importance only to rhythm is the percussion section's function of underlining the dynamics. The imaginative contrasting of louds and softs, crescendi and diminuendi, etc. is the most effective way that the drummer can communicate his feeling for the music. By the same token, there is nothing less musical than percussion which stays on the same volume level throughout a whole piece (or even a whole concert!). Don't be afraid of *ff* or *sfz*. The composer wanted the percussion to be powerful at such points.

Accents

The rhythmic security of the whole ensemble is strengthened when the percussion emphasizes the natural accents and exaggerates the artificial (written in) accents.

The accent marks within parentheses in the following rhythmic figures indicate where the natural emphasis would occur in each given bar.

Solo bass drum booms and cymbal crashes are usually marked with an accent, and these notes should be played *sfz* with *full* power.

Stickwork

The instruments of percussion which are played with sticks, hammers, or mallets in both hands utilize the natural and efficient basic technique of alternating the sticks. In rudimental snare drum parlance this is called "hand-to-hand" playing. There are many exceptions to this principle, however. The term "rudimental drumming" applies to snare drumming only. The principles of rudimental stickwork do not apply to other instruments of percussion to any great extent, but for the snare drum the alternation of single strokes is *the* very fundamenal rudiment. Because this hand-to-hand principle of stickwork dominates, we may draw up the following rules for snare drum stickwork:

The right stick leads. There are two widely used systems of snare drum stickwork: 1) the strict alternation of R (Right Hand) and L (Left Hand), starting with either hand; 2) the "*right-lead*" system of sticking for snare drum. The latter is a policy of sticking which puts a right stick on the first beat in a measure, and on all strong and principally accented beats. Weak beats, pick-up beats, and such fractional parts of beats as the eighth note off the beat are played by the left. The right-lead stickwork system can be likened to the normal bowing patterns of string instruments: the R stick corresponds to the down-bow, the L stick to the up-bow. The right-lead system is recommended. Its advantages are: it is *a system,* and hence preferable to the haphazard stick indications given in many method books; it has few exceptions in duple meters, some in triple (3/4, 3/8, 9/8); this system is based on practical performance practices and not on a "strengthen-the-left-hand" theory.

Idiomatic figures of snare drum rhythm are always played with the same sticking. By adhering to this principle, stickwork is soon eliminated as a problem, and thus sight-reading becomes easier. Improved rhythmic precision usually results when little or none of the player's conscious focus is directed to stick-work. In the case of young beginning players, it is strongly recommended that the habit of playing the typical snare drum rhythms consistently with the same sticking be developed from the start. See pages 37 to 40 for a more complete discussion of snare drum stickwork.

Rhythm, Beat, Tempo and Time

One of the most basic functions of the percussion is to provide a rhythmic foundation for the ensemble. This is especially evident in music with a regularly recurring beat such as marches, dance-like pieces, and jazz. The percussion in such cases performs the function of establishing and holding the beat.

The percussion player, therefore, should have or develop a metronomic "beat-sense" in order to time his sounds with precision. Secondly, he must possess a fine sensitivity to rhythmic patterns. He must be able to maintain a steady tempo over a long time span. In short, rhythmic precision is expected of the percussion section. Three important factors in this matter of rhythmic precision are:

1. The beginning student must concentrate from the very start on the perfecting of his "beat-sense." In all his playing he should feel the pulse of the beat to the point of exaggeration. Physical manifestations in addition to counting aloud, toe tapping, and other bodily movements usually help to make the student "beat-conscious" and should be encouraged. Needless to say, these devices should not be carried over into public performances.
2. Precision in timing requires fine neuromuscular coordination. Mechanical mastery over problems of stick control must be developed before truly fine timing is possible.
3. The recognition, comprehension, and execution of rhythm, i.e., *groupings* of beats and *divisions* within a beat, is not the exclusive province of the percussion player, yet he is properly looked upon as a specialist in matters of rhythm.

FUNCTIONS OF THE PERCUSSION INSTRUMENTS

The Percussion Section (Fr. batterie, It. batteria, Ger. Schlagewerk)

The percussion section in the modern orchestra usually consists of a timpanist, a snare drummer, a bass drummer, a cymbal specialist, and a mallet-instrument specialist. Very often one or more all-around performers are included. The concert band percussion section usually includes a timpanist, two snare drummers, a bass drummer, a cymbal player, and a mallet-instrument player, and sometimes one or more additional players. The marching band section varies in make-up with the size of the band. The large marching units employ one or two bass drummers, one or two cymbal players, four to six snare drummers, two tenor drummers, and one or two bell-lyra players.

In each of these ensembles there is considerable variation. For example, a symphonic orchestra sometimes needs to augment its basic section in order to meet the requirements of particular compositions. The make-up of the band percussion section will vary depending upon the size of the band.

One of the most important functions of the orchestra or band percussion section is that of providing a *rhythmic basis* for the ensemble. This function is most obvious in march and dance-like music, but is nearly always present to some extent. Perfect rhythm (precision in time) is to be expected of the percussionists.

The second main function of the percussion is that of *underlining dynamic nuance.* The possibilities for shading the volume of sound in the percussion instruments are probably greater than in brass, woodwinds, or strings.

The third task for the percussion section is the *providing of a variety of tone color* to the total ensemble timbre. Beginning with the introduction of the kettledrums into the orchestra, c. 1670, composers have become increasingly aware of the coloristic possibilities of percussion instruments. Rimsky-Korsakov, Ravel, Debussy, Stravinsky, and Bartók are among the nineteenth and early twentieth century composers who have exploited percussion timbre. Much contemporary music places the timbre function above rhythmic and dynamic usage, as witness certain works by Boulez, Nono, and Berio, to name but a few.

The Percussion Ensemble. In recent years a growing body of literature has appeared utilizing the percussion group of instruments as a true ensemble. Percussion ensemble music is now available for every school, college, and professional level. Chavez' *Toccata for Percussion* and *Ionisation* by Varèse are classics in this field.

At the school level, experience in small ensemble playing is now possible for percussion students through the use of graded percussion ensemble literature. Balancing of parts, rhythmic precision, and subtleties of shading can be developed by percussionists working together in an ensemble.

Percussion in Dance Music and Jazz

One of the earliest functions of the drums was to furnish a repetitive beat to accompany dancers. With the development in America of the dance orchestra came a series of inventions which enabled the bass drum, cymbals, snare drum, and other percussion instruments to be manipulated by a single player. Early jazz bands used the drums mainly as a time-beating adjunct which worked in close cooperation with the bass, piano, guitar, and other chord instruments to form the *rhythm section*. Since about 1940 there has been a trend toward setting the drums free from their monotonous duty of time-beating. The progressive jazz drummer today functions more as an equal partner with the other instruments in melodic and solo rhythmic "fill-ins" than merely as a keeper of the beat.

Since dance band and jazz combo experience form a part of most high school music programs, it behooves the instrumental music director to keep abreast of the tremendous strides which are being made in the field of dance band, stage band, and jazz drumming. The author believes that all percussion students should be given training and on-the-job experience in this idiom. The rhythmic drive and precision acquired through jazz playing is a requisite and valuable skill in all areas of percussion playing. In addition, the interest of young percussion students can often be stimulated and maintained by dance band experience.

Soloistic Possibilities. Nearly all of the major percussion instruments can be used in solo roles. The most satisfactory solo instrument of the percussion family is the marimba, which has a more mellow and resonant tone than its close relative, the xylophone, and lends itself to four-mallet chordal style. Several composers have written important works for the solo marimba, such as Paul Creston's *Concertino for Marimba and Orchestra*, Robert Kurka's *Concerto for Marimba and Orchestra*, and Darius Milhaud's *Concerto for Marimba, Vibes, and Orchestra*.

Among the drum group, the snare drum is the traditional solo instrument. A great wealth of solo material is available, chiefly of a rudimental nature designed to display the drummer's technique and command of the rudiments. Extended drum solos are difficult to justify on musical grounds, but most drum competitions and festivals admit only rudimental style solos. It is to be hoped that a more worthy musical literature will be developed which will elevate the status of snare drum solo performance.

The timpani solo literature is, happily, of a more musical nature. Some excellent accompanied and unaccompanied pieces have been written in recent years, ranging in difficulty from very easy to virtuoso level. Tcherepnin's *Sonatina for Three Timpani and Piano* (*Orchestra*), Weinberger's *Concerto*, Elliot Carter's *Improvisation for Timpani*, and Gutche's *Timpani Concertante*, Op. 31 are examples of large scale solo works. Robert Muczynski's *Three Designs for Three Timpani* was written expressly for the high school timpani soloist.

Multi-percussion solos for the individual percussionist are available, also. These works are exciting to perform and to hear. They provide a fine challenge to those individuals striving to become the "complete or total percussionist."

MUSICIANSHIP IN PERCUSSION PLAYING

Goal of Instruction Is Musicianship

In teaching percussion students the techniques of the various instruments, one must emphasize continually that beyond mere technical competence lies a higher goal—namely, *musicianship*. Highly paid professional players in symphony, jazz, recording, and theater work are masters of their craft in a technical sense, true. But they are more than technicians. In nearly every case their outstanding qualification is their basic musical feeling, which can truly be called artistry.

Can the elements which constitute musicianship be taught? The answer is *yes*, provided, of course, that the student is responsible, alert, and willing to persevere and that the instructor himself possesses and communicates thorough musicianship.

There are certain specific aspects of musicianship which the teacher and the student should check on in their day-to-day, month-to-month work. Musical playing is not mystery, nor a divine gift, nor simply long experience. Rather it can be conceived as a complex of factors which can be isolated and pursued as specific goals of instruction. Constant careful attention to the following factors of musicianship, plus the factor of practical, on-the-job experience, is the foundation upon which good percussion playing (and teaching) rests. A good musician develops and possesses:

1. Sensitivity to the expressive quality of music.

2. Sensitivity to sounds (the natural sounds as well as strictly musical).
3. The urge to experiment with sounds (at a high level: improvise, compose).
4. The urge to analyze patterns of organized sound (*hearing* music).
5. A keen sense of pitch.
6. A keen sense of time (tempo, rhythm).
7. A keen sense of timbre (color).
8. A keen sense of volume (dynamics).
9. A knowledge of tonal expectancies (progressions of tones, resolutions, logic of tones in motion).
10. A sense of tonality (key feeling, tonal center).
11. An acquaintance with the literature (*all* styles and historical periods).
12. The ability to discriminate (criticize music).
13. A knowledge of performance practices and traditions.
14. Solo and ensemble performance skill.
15. Skill in reading music.
16. The ability to memorize music.
17. Skill in following a conductor.
18. The ability to recognize and be cognizant of musical lines (phrases).

Of these facets of general musicianship, the most important for the percussionist are:

1. Sensitivity to time, rhythm, "beat-sense," tempo feeling.
2. Sensitivity to dynamics.
3. Sensitivity to timbre differences.
4. Urge to experiment with sounds.
5. Skill in reading music.
6. Skill in following a conductor.
7. The ability to recognize and be cognizant of musical lines (phrases).

Unfortunately, many percussionists are guilty of ignoring item 7 of the above listing. In their formative years of training, string, wind, and brass players are continually made aware of the necessity for accurate phrase interpretation. All too often, percussionists are permitted to concentrate on individual notes and idiomatic rhythmic figures failing to realize their obligation, along with the other instrumentalists, to contribute to the forming of complete musical statements (phrases). Playing the "musical line" is an absolute necessity for the percussionist performing contemporary literature.

Technical Facility as Means to Musical Ends

Some progress toward musical drumming has been made in this country. In most of our school music programs, however, most percussion instruction is limited to technique. Evidence of this is seen in the lists of solo and ensemble literature recommended and required for contests and festivals. A large percentage of this literature is musically worthless. The chief cause of this nonmusical orientation is the overemphasis of the "Original 26 Rudiments." Too many music educators seem to feel that technical mastery of these archaic snare drum beats constitutes an adequate background for the band or orchestra percussionist. As long as this notion persists there will exist some justification for the old saw "musicians *and* drummers."

What, then, should be the relationship of technique to well-rounded percussion playing? The answer may be discovered by looking into the actual on-the-job demands made of the performing percussionist. At every level, from the elementary school band to the professional symphony orchestra, the percussion section cannot stand on technique alone. Musical percussion playing involves all of the aspects of general musicianship. The percussion problems which beset band and orchestra directors are usually more musical than technical. Matters of accenting, dynamic contrast, steadiness of tempo, proper choice of instruments, and accurate reading are common problems. Actual manipulative problems are much less frequent. There have been many cases in our symphony orchestras where wind or string players have been rather quickly and satisfactorily converted to percussion players. School music directors, in emergency situations, have often been pleasantly surprised to find that with only a minimum of practice a string or wind player can substitute for an ailing timpanist, bass drummer, or triangle player. These situations illustrate the relationship between musicianship and technique.

On the other hand, technical facility cannot be overlooked. The foregoing paragraphs are not meant to imply that technique is unimportant, or that we should de-emphasize completely the teaching and practice of snare drum rudiments, scales and arpeggios on the mallet instruments, legato rolls on the timpani. It is certainly true that fine players are masters of their instruments in a technical sense. Endless hours of practice, practice of the most monotonous and self-disciplined kind, have gone into the building of these facile techniques. The technical mastery which is so painstakingly acquired is a most valuable possession. It is valuable not for itself but because it is a *means to express musical ends* in the performance of music. It enables the player to *express his musical feeling*. Technical competence liberates the player so that all of his *attention and thought can be directed toward interpretation.*

Technique, considered as a means to musical ends, does make up a large part of the young player's instrumental study. Instruction in correct basic techniques is the responsibility of the teacher, and required home practice is pretty much confined to basic techniques with beginning students. This is practical and sound. In the band or orchestra rehearsal, however, it is the director's job to see that the techniques are applied in musically sound ways. By his attitude the skillful instructor imparts the idea that technical virtuosity is not an end in itself, but rather serves the ends of musicianly performance.

THE CLASS APPROACH TO PERCUSSION TEACHING

Values of the Class Approach

It seems hardly necessary to justify class instrumental teaching today when one considers the fine work that instrumental teachers are accomplishing by class instructional means. In addition to the important factors of ensemble experience from the start and competitive motivation, the percussion class may function very nicely as a true percussion ensemble. Once the basic snare drum techniques have been worked out on the practice pads and snare drums, simple snare drum duets, trios, and literature for snare drum, bass drum, and cymbals can be played by the class. Other instruments are added as they are studied. Additional advantages of the class approach for percussion are:

1. Rotation of the students on the various percussion instruments is workable in the class prior to actual band or orchestra experience.
2. The class approach is a good way to inculcate desirable habits of section routine and stage deportment.
3. The habit is formed of keeping one's eye on the conductor (instructor). Percussion sections often fail to maintain that all-important sight-line to the conductor's stick.
4. Students gain familiarity with the conductor's beat patterns in advance of band or orchestra membership.

Selection of Percussion Students

The selection of students for the percussion class is a problem which is largely a matter for the instructor to solve, as school situations vary greatly. If there is opportunity for a screening of applicants, some of the following suggestions may prove helpful:

1. A class of from four to eight students is easiest to work with. Twelve should be considered the maximum number.

2. The general intelligence of each student should be checked. Most schools have cumulative record cards which the teacher may consult. In the absence of I.Q. scores, a rough but quick method would be for the teacher himself to administer a short reading comprehension quiz. A word of warning, however. There is, as yet, no positive means of predicting musical success on the basis of verbal intelligence. Studies have shown that there does exist a low, but positive, correlation between musicality and intelligence.
3. Work habits, seriousness of purpose, enthusiasm, and other personality traits should be considered. Motivation and drive to attain a certain goal are probably the most important factors in the student's musical growth.
4. Marching in time to music is a quick way to spot students who have a very deficient beat-sense. Prospective drummers who are unable to march in time are best eliminated at the outset.
5. To identify students with a good beat-sense, the instructor should set a tempo in single taps with a stick or hand clap and have the student maintain that steady beat. A more refined but similar test is the duplication of various rhythm patterns dictated by the instructor.
6. Prior or current study of another instrument, particularly the piano, should be considered. This is recommended especially in recruiting timpani prospects.
7. Despite the well-meaning intentions of school administrators and counselors, the acceptance of students into the percussion class for physical therapy or psychotherapy is to be discouraged as a practice.

Drum Pads and Other Physical Equipment

Certain basic equipment is needed for properly carrying through a successful percussion class. Each student should provide himself with a practice pad and a pair of medium weight snare drum sticks. Recommended sticks are 2A or 2B. For very young students the 4A or 5A sticks are satisfactory. Avoid the so-called pencil model 7A sticks; they are much too light. The best type of practice pad is that which comes attached to an adjustable base, but these are somewhat expensive. The less expensive rubber wedge type is satisfactory and can be carried in the pocket.

Whatever physical set-up is decided upon, the instructor should allow room so that he can circulate easily among the students. It is very important that each player's practice pad be nearly belt high as he stands in playing position.

Figure 1.2 shows three set-ups which have been used effectively.

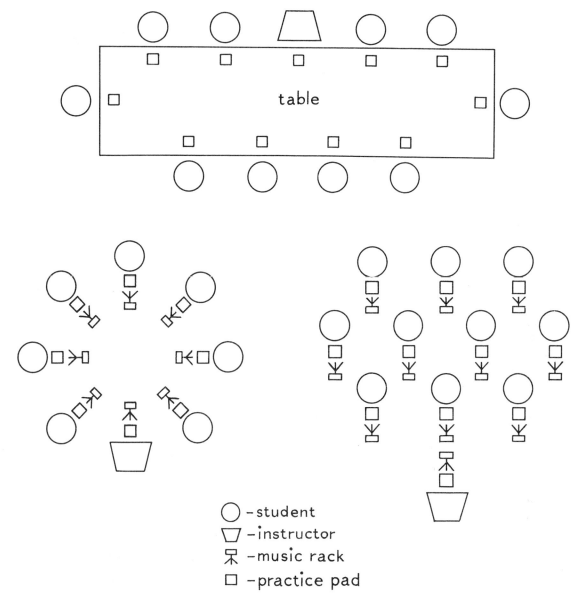

Figure 1.2. Three set-ups for beginning percussion class.

Suggested lists of basic instrumentations are given here as a guide for instructors of elementary beginning classes, junior high, and high school groups. College and university music departments should be equipped with a full inventory of standard percussion instruments.

TABLE I ELEMENTARY (BEGINNING CLASS)

Several orchestra type snare drums with stands
Bass drum
Pair of cymbals
Miscellaneous small instruments including triangle, tambourine, woodblock, castanets, etc. with a trap table

TABLE II JUNIOR HIGH SCHOOL

Several orchestra type snare drums with stands
Bass drum
Pair of cymbals
Suspended cymbal with stand
Set of bells and/or xylophone or marimba
Pair of timpani (pedal tuning)
Miscellaneous small instruments including triangle, tambourine, woodblock, castanets, etc. with trap table

TABLE III HIGH SCHOOL

Several snare drums, both orchestra and field types
Two or more tenor drums
Concert bass drum

Marching (Scotch) bass drum
One large pair of cymbals
One smaller pair of cymbals
One or two suspended cymbals with stands
Tam-tam (gong)
Set of bells
Xylophone and/or marimba
Set of tubular chimes
Three timpani (pedal tuning)
Dance band drum set
Miscellaneous small instruments including triangle, tambourine, woodblock, castanets, etc. with trap table

The set-up for a percussion class using a full complement of percussion instruments should be the same as that used in the band or orchestra percussion section.

Sequence of Studies

Since snare drum technique is basic to all percussion playing, it is the logical starting point for all players. Mastery of the snare drum handholds and arm, wrist, and hand motions makes easier the mallet played instruments and timpani technique. Practice pads should be used for the first several lessons. Snare drums should be used in the class, if available, after the first few rudiments can be played fairly well. Following the first group of lessons on essential snare drum techniques, the selected textbook should be introduced. Do not attempt the learning of reading skills until stick control is well developed.

Accurate reading of the most common snare drum figures is the second stage of percussion class study. The exercises introduced should include single strokes, taps, and flams. Reading material containing rolls should be delayed until the students can execute the long and short stroke rolls satisfactorily. Rote learning of remaining rudiments should then proceed concurrently with graded reading material. The class period at this stage should be divided between rudiment drill and reading practice.

The introduction of the bass drum and the cymbals should be made after some degree of reading skill has been achieved, and the snare drum roll can be executed fairly well. For creating interesting ensemble effects, various combinations of snare drums, bass drums, and cymbals can be used. For reading practice, this combination of instruments can make use of the drum parts to actual band and orchestra scores. Most instruction books contain many study pages scored for snare drum, bass drum, and cymbals. Later, easy percussion ensembles scored for this combination can be learned. In many elementary school situations this basic snare drum-bass drum-cymbals group will constitute a year's class work, and will enable most students in the class to proceed the next year to band or orchestra.

If the class can be continued a second year, much can be done in the areas of mallet-played instruments, timpani, and the so-called "traps" or miscellaneous small percussion instruments. Musically satisfying percussion ensemble work utilizes many instruments and so it follows that the ideal course of study would include instruction on all of the standard instruments prior to the student's enrollment in performing groups.

Since this sequence of class work is not always possible to schedule, the band and orchestra sectional rehearsals provide an alternative solution to the problem of *when* to carry out the necessary instruction for the mallet instruments, the timpani, and the small instruments.

Finally, it is realized that technical instruction is a day-to-day process carried on within the framework of full band and orchestra rehearsals. Conscientious instructors and students can make application of much of the material of the *Guide* while working out specific problems encountered in the music being studied. Individual practice of techniques is, of course, required for real mastery.

The foregoing paragraphs have dealt with the class instructional approach as it may be applied to the learning of percussion instruments. The realities of school music life being what they are, most work must necessarily be carried on in large groups. Good results can be achieved by this means, especially with the snare drum. However, the rather specialized techniques of the xylophone, marimba, vibraharp, and especially the timpani, indicate private instruction whenever and wherever a *competent* teacher can be found. Because a school normally has access to only one set of bells, one xylophone, one pair of timpani, etc., it is somewhat of a problem to carry on advanced work on these instruments in a class setting.

CHAPTER 2

Functional Classification
of Percussion Instruments

System of Classification

Historical and pedagogical literature contains varied and confusing classifications of the numerous percussion instruments. Starting from the basic definition of percussion instruments as *those musical instruments whose sound is produced by striking*, writers have offered differing systems for subgrouping this large and extremely heterogeneous family.

Curt Sachs[1] classifies percussion instruments under two headings, membranophones and idiophones. The membranophones basically are drums, whose construction includes one or two stretched membranes (skins, heads). The shells may be of wood, metal, bamboo, gourd, etc. and their general shapes are tubular, kettle (hemispheric), and frame. Plates and bars are used in the construction of the idiophones, which are instruments made of naturally sonorous substances not requiring additional tension as do membranes. Idiophones can be made of metal, wood, plastic or composition, and assume a variety of shapes like plates, tubes, rods, strips, blocks, and bars. Some idiophones, like the pair of cymbals, are played by striking together while others are struck with sticks, mallets, or rods. Further differentiation is made between an idiophonic instrument like the xylophone which is a set of bars, or plates, and others, like the triangle, which are single rods, or bars. Still other idiophones are sounded by means of shaking (maracas), scraping (guiro), and friction (sandpaper blocks).

A somewhat more useful system for classifying the instruments of percussion has been adopted by writers on musical acoustics[2,3,4] who find it convenient to subgroup the instruments according to *whether or not they emit a definite pitch*. Thus the timpani, xylophone, marimba, vibraphone, bells, and chimes would fall into one category while the bass drum, snare drum, cymbals, tam-tam, triangle, and the dozens of more primitive and exotic instruments would fall into the non-pitch category. Percussionists take exception, however, to the acousticians' relegation of the non-pitched instruments to the status of mere noisemakers.

Because each of the sonorous materials commonly used in constructing the instruments of percussion produces a unique and identifiable timbre, composers and orchestrators often think of the percussion family as made up of three subgroups: the membranes (including all the drum-type instruments), the metals (including the cymbals, tam-tam or gong, triangle, bells, vibraphone, chimes), and woods (xylophone, marimba, woodblock, temple blocks, and various gourd instruments).

The most practical classification of the percussion instruments is derived from their functions in the orchestra and band and their general manner of playing. Thus, a table may be drawn up as follows:

I. Drums with definite pitch:
   timpani (kettledrums)
II. Drums with indefinite pitch:
   snare drum
   field dum
   tenor drum
   tambour de Provence
   tom-tom
   bass drum
III. Cymbals:
   pair of clash or hand cymbals
   suspended cymbals
      sizzle
      Chinese
      swish

[1]Sachs, Curt, *History of Musical Instruments*, New York, Norton & Co., Inc., 1940.
[2]Bartholomew, W. T., *Acoustics of Music*, New York, Prentice-Hall, Inc., 1942.
[3]Culver, Charles A., *Musical Acoustics*, Philadelphia, The Blakiston Co., 1947.
[4]Backus, John, *The Acoustical Foundations of Music*, New York, Norton & Co., 9 1969.

   sock cymbals (hi-hat, afterbeat, etc.)
   antique cymbals (crotales)
   finger cymbals
IV. Mallet-played instruments:
   xylophone
   marimba
   vibraphone (vibraharp)
   bells (glockenspiel, orchestra bells, campanelli)
   chimes
   bell-lyra
V. Miscellaneous percussion instruments, including the so-called "traps" and sound-effects:
   triangle
   tambourine (tambour de Basque)
   tam-tam (gong)
   woodblock
   castanets
   metal castanets
   Chinese temple blocks
   anvil
   auto horn (claxon)
   ratchet (raganella, crécelle)
   sandpaper blocks
   siren
   slapstick (whip)
   sleighbells
   thunder sheet
   wind machine
   steel plate
   brake drum
   horse hooves (coconut shells)
   bird whistles (cuckoo, canary, etc.)

   lion roar (string drum)
   dog bark (puita)
   police whistle
   jingles
   marching machine
VI. Latin-American rhythm instruments:
   claves
   maracas (shakers)
   guiro (notched gourd, reco-reco)
   cowbell (cencerro)
   bongos
   timbales
   quijada (jawbone)
   conga drum (tumba, tumbadora)
   chacalho (metal shaker)
   casaba (gourd shaker with rattles)
VII. Dance band drum set:
   small bass drum (22″ x 14″) with foot pedal beater
   small snare drum (5½″ x 14″)
   sock cymbals (hi-hat, afterbeat) with pedal mechanism
   crash cymbal (17″ or 18″ diameter)
   small tom-tom (9″ x 13″)
   large tom-tom (16″ x 16″)
   cowbell

A comprehensive reference table follows which lists the instruments of percussion with their French, Italian, and German equivalent designations, basic techniques, acoustical features, and characteristic usages.

I DRUMS

	ACOUSTICAL FEATURES	BASIC TECHNIQUE	CHARACTERISTIC USAGES
Timpani (kettledrums) Fr. timbales It. timpani Ger. pauken	Head may be tuned to definite pitches by hand screws, pedals, chain or other mechanism. The greater the tension on the head the higher the pitch. Head vibrates as a whole and in segments. The vibration is resonated by the hollow hemispherical metal shells, called bowls.	Striking the heads with various types of timpani sticks which have felt-covered, felt disc, or wooden ends. Tones sustained by means of single stroke roll.	In classical music the pair of timpani were tuned to the tonic and dominant of the tonality and reinforced the bass line and brass passages. Beginning with Beethoven, tunings other than tonic and dominant were used, and solo passages given to the timpani. Nineteenth century composers scored for three, four and more timpani, and called for rapid changes of pitch. The modern timpanist requires at least four machine-tuned timpani and at times as many as six.
Snare Drum (side drum) Fr. caisse claire It. piccolo cassa Ger. kleinetrommel	Top (batter) head tuned very tight, bottom (snare) head not quite as tight. Vibration from batter head is transferred to snare head. The gut or wire snares rattle crisply against the snare head. As in all two-headed drums, the diameter governs the pitch (highness or lowness) and the depth of the shell governs the volume (loudness).	Striking the top (batter) head with snare drumsticks. T o n e sustained by means of rapidly alternating double strokes, called the *roll*.	Marking rhythm figures, especially repetitive march and dance patterns. Underlining dynamics, often by means of the roll.
Field Drum (parade drum, street drum) Fr. tambour militaire It. tamburo militare Ger. militartrommel 	Same as for snare drum, except that shell is proportionately deeper.	Same as for snare drum.	Playing marching beats. In concert music used when deep and military snare drum tone is indicated.
Tenor Drum Fr. caisse roulante It. cassa rullante Ger. ruhrtrommel 	Top and bottom head, but no snares. Both the diameter and depth of shell are greater than those of the snare drums.	Same as for snare drum and field drum, except that in marching band and drum corps, hard felt-ended sticks are used.	Very much like a tom-tom in sound. Used in marching bands and drum corps to furnish a sound midway in depth between the snare drum and the bass drum.

Tambour de Provence (Fr. only)

Top and bottom heads, but with only one thick cord (snare) under bottom head.

Striking with large snare drumsticks.

Called for only in French scores. Bizet's *L'Arlésienne Suite* is an instance. Also used in Milhaud's *Suite Francaise*.

Tom-tom

Top and bottom heads which are tunable. Sizes range from 7″ x 13″ to 18″ x 18″.

Striking the top head with snare drumsticks or hard felt sticks.

Used chiefly in the dance band drum set-up. Also used to imitate primitive or exotic drums in concert music.

Bass Drum
Fr. grosse caisse
It. gran cassa, cassa grande
Ger. grosse trommel

Size varies with type of ensemble in which it is used. Both heads tuned fairly loosely, so that very lowest frequencies predominate. No definite pitch is desirable.

Playing surface is struck with single or double-ended bass drum beater. Parade (Scotch) bass drum played with two hard felt beaters, one in either hand. Dance band bass drum played by means of a foot pedal. Bass drum roll is produced by using two timpani sticks.

Marks the strong beats in march and dance music. Underlines the dynamics in other types of music. Provides the lowest frequencies to reinforce the bass instruments. Dramatic use of solo "booms" and rolls is common.

II. CYMBALS

Cymbals (pair of clashed cymbals)
Fr. cymbales
It. piatti
     cinelli
Ger. becken

ACOUSTICAL FEATURES

A good pair of cymbals are matched to complement one another in order to bring out the greatest number of frequencies. This simultaneous sounding of a wide range of frequencies accounts for the brilliant, crashy tone characteristic of fine cymbals.

BASIC TECHNIQUE

The cymbals are held by means of loose rawhide straps and are sounded by clashing one against the other.

CHARACTERISTIC USAGES

Cymbals are ancient instruments which were brought into the orchestra during the classic period. (Mozart-*Abduction from the Seraglio*; Haydn-*Military Symphony*) being at that time chiefly associated with Turkish military music. Subsequent composers have employed the cymbals mainly to add brilliancy to the band and orchestra timbre, and to help in marking the rhythm in marches and dance music.

Suspended cymbal

Fr. cymbale suspendé
    cymbale libre
It. piatto sospeso
Ger. becken frei

The sound of cymbals varies with their diameter and thickness. In the case of the suspended cymbal a third very important variable is the choice of beater. Each type of beater brings out a different set of frequencies. A further variable is the playing spot, i.e, edge, top, or dome.

Variations in construction and additions to the regular suspended cymbal create further variable sounds such as attaching rivets at its circumference (sizzle cymbal), having the edges turned up with a squarer crown (Chinese cymbal), or combining both of the above (swish cymbal).

The single cymbal is mounted on a floor stand which allows it to vibrate freely. It can be struck with mallets, drumsticks, timpani sticks, wire brushes, triangle beater, or even a coin.

Used chiefly for very dry, choked crashes and, by means of a single stroke roll, for assisting in creating tremendous crescendi. A characteristic rhythm figure

[musical notation]

is played by dance and jazz drummers on the top of a large suspended cymbal, using the right stick or brush.

Sock cymbals (high-hat, afterbeat cymbals)

The characteristic sound is a "ching" or "chup" as the cymbals contact each other.

The sock cymbal set-up consists of a pair of 14" or 15" cymbals clashed by means of a foot pedal mechanism. Sticks or brushes can be used on the top or edges while the cymbals are being operated by the left foot.

Used in dance music and jazz exclusively. In 4/4 measure it is played on the afterbeats, using the left foot. The rhythm figure

[musical notation]

is sometimes played on the sock cymbals.

Antique cymbals

Fr. crotales
It. crotalo
Ger. antiken Zimbeln

Antique cymbals are very thick in comparison with their diameters, being essentially circular bars. They have a definite pitch, and are usually used in pairs pitched a fifth apart. They emit a clear bell-like tone.

These tiny cymbals are not struck as are regular cymbals. If both are to sound, they are struck one edge against another edge at a single point. If only one is to sound, the other cymbal is muffled by holding with the fingers. An alternative is to strike the single cymbal with a triangle beater.

Used sparingly by a few composers for coloristic purposes, (Debussy-Afternoon of a Faun). Pitches are specified in scores requiring use of antique cymbals. Some contemporary band scores such as Husa's Music for Prague 1968 call for their use.

Finger cymbals

Fr. cymbales doigts
It. cinelli dito
Ger. fingernbecken

Finger cymbals are thinner than antique cymbals. They do not emit a definite single pitch, but produce a cluster of very high frequencies with very little volume or carrying power.

Same as for antique cymbals.

Rarely called for in symphonic scores. Limited use by modern composers of small ensemble and percussion music. Berio's Circles is an example.

III. MALLET-PLAYED INSTRUMENTS

Xylophone

Fr. xylophone,
     clagnebois
It. silophono,
     sticcato
Ger. holz und
     strohinstrument
     xylophon
     strohfiedel

ACOUSTICAL FEATURES

The xylophone consists of a series of chromatically tuned wooden bars mounted on a frame. A 2½ to 4 octave range is usual, the majority of xylophones having a range of 3 octaves, c′ to c′′′′. The bars are arranged in two banks, corresponding to the piano keyboard's white and black keys. Most xylophones do not have resonators, although the so-called concert model is an exception. Typical xylophone tone quality is hard, brittle and rather piercing. The xylophone sounds one octave higher than written.

BASIC TECHNIQUE

Striking the bars with mallets, one in either hand. To sustain a note the rapidly alternating single stroke roll is used.

CHARACTERISTIC USAGES

The xylophone was at one time chiefly a solo instrument. Vaudeville era performers developed a facile and brilliant technique. In band and orchestra scores the xylophone is used sparingly, typically to play short melodic lines of a dry, angular and brittle nature.

Marimba

ACOUSTICAL FEATURES

Prototype marimbas developed both in Africa and South America. There is a certain similarity of appearance to the xylophone, but the marimba's tone quality is more mellow due to the wider and flatter wooden bars, and also to the softer mallets used. An additional feature is the resonating tube mounted beneath each bar to aid in amplifying and sustaining the sound. Range is usually from c to c′′ or c′′′′.

BASIC TECHNIQUE

Striking the bars with mallets (normally softer than xylophone mallets), one in either hand. Chordal style used in solo playing employs two mallets in each hand. The roll is the same as that of the xylophone.

CHARACTERISTIC USAGES

The marimba is widely used as a solo instrument. In the low register it can sound almost organ-like when played with the four-mallet tremolo. The marimba does not have the penetrating tone quality of the xylophone, and for this reason is seldom used in band and orchestra. However, concerti for marimba and orchestra have been written by Creston and Kurka.

Vibraphone (vibraharp)

It. vibrafono

ACOUSTICAL FEATURES

The "vibe" has the same keyboard layout as the wood-barred instruments, but the bars are made of a metal alloy. The most distinctive features of the vibraphone are a sustaining pedal which is operated by the foot, and the electrically driven "vibrato" mechanism which consists of discs on a shaft which alternately open and close the resonating tubes. Range is usually from f to f′′.

BASIC TECHNIQUE

Techniques are basically like those of the xylophone and marimba, except that the tremolo (roll) is not needed to sustain tones. Instead, the damper pedal is used as it is in piano playing.

CHARACTERISTIC USAGES

In concert music the vibraphone is employed mainly to play bell tones, chords and arpeggios. In jazz the instrument has become a popular solo and ensemble instrument, often used without the "vibra" to produce a sound which is cooler and less lush than its normal quality.

Bells (orchestra bells)

Fr. jeu de timbres
    jeu de clochettes
It. campanelli
Ger. glockenspiel

The small metal bars are mounted as in the other mallet-played instruments. Most models do not have resonators, although the so-called Parsifal bells are an exception. Rubber tipped mallets of various degrees of hardness are used, as are metal disc type beaters. The tones sustain and tend to produce a clang when bell tones are sounded in quick succession. The bells have a range of 2½ octaves from written g to c′′ sounding two octaves higher.

Technique basically same as for xylophone and marimba.

Bell tones, singly or in octaves, arpeggios, and diatonic melodic lines are common.

Chimes

Fr. cloches
It. campani
Ger. glocken

The metal tubes sound somewhat like carillon bells, but have fewer overtones. The tones sustain themselves so long that rapid passages sound blurred. Chimes equipped with a damper pedal make hand damping unnecessary, but for the other type, damping is the main problem. Control of the volume is another problem.

The top ends of the tubes are struck at an angle with a laminated wood or chamois covered chime mallet. Some passages require two mallets. The more recent models are equipped with a damper pedal to help overcome the problem of discordant clang.

Single bell tones, church bell effects, and repetitive arpeggiated figures are common.

Bell-lyra (glockenspiel)

Same as for bells.

This marching band version of the orchestra bells is held in a sling in front of the player with the keyboard extending from low to high in the direction of march. Two pyralin or hard rubber mallets are used.

The bell-lyra doubles the melodic line in marching band music.

IV. MISCELLANEOUS PERCUSSION INSTRUMENTS

	ACOUSTICAL FEATURES	BASIC TECHNIQUE	CHARACTERISTIC USAGES
Triangle Fr. triangle It. triangolo Ger. triangel 	Experimentation will show on which leg and at what point to strike the triangle for the purest tone. Several sizes and diameters of triangles are needed to fill the concert repertoire requirements. In very soft playing the triangle is struck very close to its upper corner. Various weights of beaters produce varying tone qualities.	The triangle is suspended by a narrow gut string attached to a clamp which is detached from the music rack and held about head high for playing position. The metal beater rod may strike the outside of the right leg of the triangle or the inner side of the lower leg. A roll can be executed by rapid alternating strokes between closed ends of the triangle.	This very ancient instrument came into the orchestra along with the cymbals during the eighteenth century. It is a coloristic instrument, contributing a delicate and ethereal timbre to the ensemble. Sometimes it is used simply to add a dash of metallic sound to the drum timbre.
Tambourine Fr. tambour de Basque It. tamburo basco tamburino Ger. becken tambourin	The tone quality of a tambourine is dependent upon the diameter, the tension of the head, and the number of jingles attached. The tambourine is a hybrid, being partly drum and partly tiny pairs of cymbals.	For ordinary playing, the tambourine is held in the left hand and its head is rapped sharply by the fingers and thumb of the right hand formed into a small tight ball of flesh. The roll is produced either by shaking with a rotating wrist motion, or by moistening the right thumb tip and rubbing it around the outer perimeter of the tambourine head.	In modern scores the tambourine is used chiefly for the sake of its individual sound in marking the rhythm. In light concert music it is often used when a Spanish or Gypsy flavor is desired. The tambourine is also used in the Brazilian samba.
Tam-tam (gong) Fr. tam-tam It. tam-tam Ger. tam-tam	A circular, slightly convex metallic disk with the edges turned inward, the tamtam or gong (in modern day symphonic organizations, these terms are used interchangeably) may range in size from ten to forty inches in diameter. Naturally, the larger instruments will produce a darker, more resonant sound. The larger instruments do not "speak" quickly, the tone seeming to reach its maximum volume a second or two after impact. The after-ring is lengthy and careful damping is necessary.	The tam-tam is struck with a large heavy chamois or felt covered beater which is usually weighted with lead. Most tamtams sound best when struck a few inches off center.	Although the tam-tam still suggests the Orient, it is now called for in scores of all types. The sound is serious and awesome. Loud gong crashes are often used to mark a climax.

Woodblock

Fr. bois
It. legno
Ger. holz

The best resonance is obtained from a block about 8" long and 2½" deep. The two sides are slotted to produce differing tones.

The woodblock may be held at one end and struck with a single xylophone mallet or drumstick on its top surface, or it may be placed on the trap table and played with two sticks. The tips or the shoulders of the snare drumstick may be used, depending upon the volume and tone quality desired.

The woodblock is mainly a color effect and is suggestive of Oriental music. It is also used to suggest "ricky-tick" vaudeville and early Dixieland orchestras.

Castanets

Fr. castagnettes
It. castagnetta
Ger. kastagnetten

The main problem is to control the castanets so that unwanted extra notes will not blur the rhythm.

Percussionists do not attempt to play the castanets in the manner of the Spanish dancers. Instead, the shells of the castanets are mounted opposite one another separated by a broad wooden handle. When the handle is shaken in mid-air against the opposite hand or against the knee, the castanets sound. A better arrangement is to have the castanet shells attached by a spring to a piece of resonant wood so that they can be played by striking with the fingertips or with drumsticks.

Castanets are used almost without exception for the purpose of imparting a Spanish flavor to a composition or arrangement. Repetitive rhythm figures are typical.

Metal Castanets

Fr. castagnettes de fer
It. castagnetta ferra
Ger. metallkastgnetten

Metal castanets are finger cymbals mounted opposite each other so that they can be clashed together by squeezing the hand spring.

The pair of metal castanets is played by striking the flat surfaces against each other, preferably by means of a spring-type holder.

Repetitive rhythm figures are typical. The metal castanets do not produce as dry a sound as the wooden type, nor do they suggest a Spanish flavor.

INSTRUMENTS

Temple blocks (Chinese temple blocks)

ACOUSTICAL FEATURES

Usually a set consists of five blocks, each with a different pitch. The pitches are indefinite, but unmistakably "higher" or "lower."

BASIC TECHNIQUE

The set of blocks is mounted with the lower pitched blocks to the left. They may be struck with xylophone mallets, felt timpani sticks or snare drumsticks.

CHARACTERISTIC USAGES

The temple blocks are another import from the Orient, and have been used to suggest Oriental atmosphere and as horsehoof imitations.

Anvil
Fr. enclume
It. incudine
Ger. amboss

Some anvils sound best when struck on the tongue or tapered end. A section of railroad track will often give a heavy metallic sound much superior to that of the anvil. Percussion equipment companies have available for sale "concert anvils" consisting of a metal bar and beater. These are compact, easy to transport, and produce a very fine metallic sound.

The anvil is usually struck on its top surface with a small ball pein or regular hammer.

Very limited call in the repertoire for the anvil. Its sound is suggestive of great force, fury, armor and battle. Verdi–*Il Trovatore* is a classic example. A modern work calling for anvil is Gene Gutche's *Holofernes Overture.*

Auto horn (claxon)

———

Pressing down the lever sounds the horn. In the bulb type of horn, a sudden squeezing of the rubber bulb sounds the horn.

Limited to descriptive music portraying traffic sounds. Gershwin–*An American in Paris* is an example.

Ratchet
Fr. crécelle
It. raganella
Ger. handratsche

To maintain a steady volume of sound it is necessary to turn the handle at a constant rate.

The ratchet clamp is usually attached to the bass drum hoop. To sound the ratchet, turn the handle clockwise.

This curious sound effect has been used by many composers in a variety of idioms. It has no clear associative or imitative qualities. Example is Honnegger –*Jeanne d'Arc.*

Sandpaper blocks

The blocks should be about as large as can comfortably be grasped in the hands to give the maximum volume. Medium or fine sandpaper is best.

One block is held stationary, the other brushed against it in rhythm.

Limited to train and steamboat imitations and soft shoe rhythms.

Siren
Fr. sirène
It. sirèno
Ger. sirene

———

The small type used by theater drummers is held in the mouth and blown with the breath. The large fire sirens used in certain symphonic works are cranked.

Usually confined to funny music and descriptive background music. Most serious use of the large siren in Varèse – *Ionisation.*

INSTRUMENTS	ACOUSTICAL FEATURES	BASIC TECHNIQUE	CHARACTERISTIC USAGES
Slapstick Fr. fouet It. frusta Ger. peitsche	—	The action is similar to an actual whip crack in the case of the commonly used type of slapstick. Another model has two handles by means of which the two boards can be slapped shut.	Used in certain descriptive pieces.
Sleighbells Fr. grelots It. sonagli Ger. schellen	To play softly, contact several of the bells with the hands. This allows only two or three to vibrate.	The most convenient way to play rhythm figures cleanly on sleighbells is to have them mounted on a flat board, which can then be shaken up and down.	Highly suggestive of sleigh rides, Christmas, Santa Claus, etc. Most serious use in Mahler–*Fourth Symphony*.
Thunder sheet	—	A large sheet of metal is shaken to produce the thunder imitation.	Used to imitate thunder.
Wind machine	—	This barrel-like machine is cranked to provide a friction sound which rises and falls in pitch with changes in the rate of cranking.	Wind imitation. Most serious use is in Strauss–*Don Quixote*.
Steel plate	—	The plate is suspended with a heavy gut or cord, and struck with a metal beater such as a bell mallet or a small hammer.	Steeple bell imitations, fire alarm effects, and occasionally in modern scores they are employed simply for their own timbre. An example of the latter is Dorati–*Missa Brevis*.
Brake drum	Certain brake drums have a very beautiful, clear and resonant sound.	Can be struck with metal bell mallets or a small hammer.	An ethereal and other-worldly sound.

INSTRUMENTS

INSTRUMENTS	BASIC TECHNIQUE / ACOUSTICAL FEATURES	CHARACTERISTIC USAGES
Horse hooves (coconut shells)	The best horsehoof imitation consists of two coconut shells fitted with leather handles at their tops. These are clapped against a marble base in the characteristic rhythm.	Horsehoof imitations.
Bird whistles	The canary imitation must be filled with water prior to use. In the type known as the cuckoo whistle, a plunger controls the pitch.	Literal bird call imitations.
Lion roar (string drum)	A single headed drum rather bucket-like in appearance, mounted on a base with a rosined string fastened through the head at its center. When a piece of leather is drawn along the string it causes the head to vibrate to sound like a lion's roar.	Imitation of lion's roar. Example is Ganz–*Percussion Melange*.
Dog bark (Portuguese—*puita*)	Instrument consists of a hollow box, the top side of which is rosined and then moved back and forth sharply across the top of the box to create a frictional vibration.	Imitation of dog's bark. Most serious use is Villa-Lobos—*Choros #10*.
ACOUSTICAL FEATURES	**BASIC TECHNIQUE**	**CHARACTERISTIC USAGES**
Police whistle	Whistle is blown forcibly with the breath.	Traffic noise sound effect. Ibert's *Divertissment* contains notes for the police whistle.
Jingles It. sonaglieri	Consists of a pair of tambourine jingles mounted at the end of a rattan handle. Played by tapping against the knee.	A pair of jingles is called for in Vaughn-Williams – *London Symphony*.

Marching machine

This box-like machine is cranked to allow blocks inside to fall against a sounding board.

Imitation of troops on the march.

V. LATIN AMERICAN INSTRUMENTS

Claves (Spanish)

BASIC TECHNIQUE

One clave is held by the finger tips of the cupped left hand. The other is held lightly in the right hand. The right clave strikes the left on top, over the center of the left palm.

ACOUSTICAL FEATURES

The cupped hand acts as a sound box. Both claves must be held very lightly in order to obtain maximum resonance.

CHARACTERISTIC USAGES

The claves beat is the basis of most of the Latin-American dance rhythms. It is usually one of the following repetitive two-measure phrases:

Maracas (Spanish)

BASIC TECHNIQUE

Shaking alternately, usually with an up and down motion, the rhythm of straight eighth notes.

ACOUSTICAL FEATURES

Dried seeds, shot or tiny pebbles are used as the filler material which rattles against the sides of the gourd.

CHARACTERISTIC USAGES

Basic instrument (along with the claves) of the Latin-American dance rhythms. Used in the rhumba, bolero, cha-cha-cha, mambo, meringue, samba (both maracas held in one hand in samba rhythm).

INSTRUMENTS

Guiro (Spanish)
Gourd (English), also called rasper, scratcher, guaracha, reco-reco

BASIC TECHNIQUE

Sounded by scraping across the notched surface with a stiff wire set in a handle, with a stick, or even a comb.

ACOUSTICAL FEATURES

The volume of sound is controlled by the speed and pressure of the scraping action plus the type of scraper used.

CHARACTERISTIC USAGES

Used mainly in sambas, but can also be used in the Cuban dance forms. Villa-Lobos, Varèse, and Stravinsky have scored for guiro.

Cowbell (English)
Cencerro (Spanish)

Can be held in one hand and struck with a snare drumstick, or attached by means of a clamp to a stand or to the bass drum hoop.

The cowbell produces a loud "bonk" when struck with the shoulder of the snare drumstick near its open end. A softer "tick" is made by striking the bell near its closed end using the tip of the drumstick. The cowbell should be muffled by wrapping with tape.

In Latin music, each dance has its distinctive cowbell rhythm. The cowbell usually maintains a one or two measure pattern, changing only at the end of definite sections. At times it may be utilized to create its own free-style rhythmic line for added color.

Bongos (Spanish)

The small bongo should be tuned to a high pitch, the large one a fourth or more lower. The characteristic ringing "pop" on the high bongo is produced when the fingers contact the edge and the playing surface of the head simultaneously.

The pair of bongos are held between the knees, large bongo to the right. The heads are struck by the extended first and second fingers of each hand, usually at a point near the edge.

The bongos do not have a strict rhythm pattern to which they must adhere. The player is free to improvise in authentic Latin style.

Timbales (Spanish)

Timbales are a pair of metal-shelled, single headed drums mounted on a stand (sizes 6" x 13" and 6" x 14"). The sides, as well as the heads are used for producing sound. Striking the sides is called "paila" style. Although considered drums of indefinite pitch, the heads of the timbales may be tensioned to vary in pitch from a perfect fourth to a perfect fifth, as desired.

The timbales are played with cylindrical sticks, 3/8" wide by 12" long. Both sticks are held in a manner similar to the grip for the right snare stick. The player usually stands. The larger timbal is at the player's left (as opposed to the bongos).

Timbales maintain a steady beat pattern in Latin dances. Rim shot combinations are commonly used for fill-ins.

Jawbone (English) Quijada (Spanish)

The sound is caused by the loose teeth rattling in their sockets in this instrument which is simply the jawbone of an ass.

The jawbone is held in one hand and struck with the heel of palm of the other.

Used mainly in sambas. It plays the most simple of parts and is usually used only on single notes.

Conga drum (English) Tumbadora, tumba (Spanish)

A high pitched sound is made with the extended fingers striking at the edge of the head. A lower tone is made by striking with the heel of the palm near the center.

Can be suspended by means of a shoulder sling in front of the player, or set on a stand. The extended fingers and heels of the palms are used.

Used in nearly all Latin dance rhythms to provide a low pitched drum sound. The conga drum typically sounds the second quarter and final two eighths of each measure in Latin rhythms.

Shaker (English) also called metal shaker
Chocalho (Spanish)
Chucala (Portuguese)

The sound is caused by the enclosed shot rattling against the sides of the tin shaker.

The shaker is played with an up and down motion of the forearm and wrist. It may be held in the center with one hand, or held at each end with both hands.

Not one of the essential rhythm instruments, but often used in sambas. Called for in several Villa-Lobos scores.

Casaba (Spanish)

Large beads strung over the outer surface rattle against the hollow gourd.

Played by turning the gourd and slapping the beads with the opposite hand.

Used mainly in sambas and meringues.

CHAPTER 3

Snare Drum

GENERAL DESCRIPTION

The generic term *snare drum* includes drums of varying depths, diameters, and tonal qualities. Common to all are a cylindrical wood or metal shell, a calfskin or plastic head stretched over each end, and wire or gut cords called snares, which are stretched tightly across the bottom head. The drumheads are tucked over hoops, called flesh hoops and are held in place by counterhoops, called rims. Threaded rods may be turned to apply tension to the heads, and thus tune the drums. The top head is called the *batter head*, the bottom the *snare head*. When the batter head is struck with the drumsticks the air inside the drum is set into vibrations which are transferred to the snare head. The vibration of the snare head causes the snares to rattle crisply against it, thus producing the characteristic tone of the snare drum. The depth of the drum shell governs its volume and the diameter governs its pitch. The various types of musical organizations demand differing ratios of depth to diameter. A marching band therefore requires deep toned snare drums capable of producing a loud volume, while the jazz combo needs a snare drum of high pitch, crisp rather than deep toned, and relatively small volume.

TYPES OF SNARE DRUMS

The *concert snare drum* ranges in depth from 6½″ to 8″ and is 14″ or 15″ in diameter. It is used in the symphony orchestra, the concert band, and is a good general purpose drum for school orchestras and bands. The shell may be made of wood or metal. It is commonly believed that the metal shell produces a more brilliant and penetrating sound. Wire snares are widely used, and are the most practical for school use. Most concert snare drums come from the manufacturer equipped with wire snares. A majority of symphonic band and orchestra players prefer the thin gut snares because they produce a drier tone than do the wire snares. Gut snares are less responsive, however, and also require more frequent adjustment. One manufacturer now markets a combination gut-wire set of snares, which has the advantage of gut tone with wire response. The most expensive concert snare drum models have provision for individual adjustment of each snare strand. A so-called tone control device, which is mounted inside the shell and presses against the snare head when a knob is turned on the outside of the shell,

Courtesy Ludwig Drum Co.

Figure 3.1. Concert Snare Drum.

is a feature of some snare drums. The concert snare drum is mounted on a sturdy metal stand which is adjustable in height and degree of slant.

Courtesy Ludwig Drum Co.

Figure 3.2. Field Drum.

The *field, or parade, snare drum* ranges in depth from 9″ to 14″ and 13″ to 16″ in diameter. It is used primarily in drum corps and marching bands, but can be used in the concert band. Some orchestra scores call specifically for a field drum when the composer wishes to suggest the sounds of martial music. When used in marching units the drum is carried by a sling which passes over the player's right shoulder and allows the drum to ride at a slant over the left leg. Also available from various percussion companies is a device designed to hold field and tenor drums out and away from the body torso. This device, known as a "hi-stepper," allows the drummer freedom of leg and arm movement plus maximum carrying ease and control of the drum. Gut snares were formerly used on all field drums, but in recent years wire snares have become the rule rather than the exception. The field drum should be equipped with gut snares to achieve its true sound. Only for elementary age students would wire snares be advantageous, because they require less careful adjustment. Wire wound silk cord snares are still to be found occasionally, but are unsatisfactory. The combination wire-gut snares would be good for a field drum which is to be used in the concert band. For concert playing the field drum

should be mounted on a heavy duty snare drum stand.

The *dance band snare drum* is simply a small version of the concert drum. Changing conceptions of ideal tone for dance band, show, recording, and combo work have been responsible for the great variation to be found in dance drums. The trend generally has been toward a shallow, crisp, brilliant and responsive drum. Depth of tone and great volume are not needed for most pop, jazz, and recording work. The size of

Courtesy Ludwig Drum Co.

Figure 3.3. Dance Band Snare Drum.

the most widely used dance drum is 5½″ or 6″ by 14″. Dance band type drums are sometimes used in elementary school groups as concert drums, and are satisfactory for this purpose. They are not, however, at all adequate for secondary, college, or professional concert work. The shell of dance drums are constructed of either wood or metal. Most percussionists are now using the metal shell. Wire snares are best. For added responsiveness, 18 or 20 strand snare sets are often used on dance drums in contrast to the usual 12 strand sets found on most concert drums. The dance band snare drum is mounted on a stand which is adjusted to accomodate the sitting position of the player.

DRUMHEADS

Drumheads for the snare drum, historically, have been made of calfskin. In recent years, plastic heads have been replacing the calfskin heads. There was a period in their early development when the plastic heads were not too satisfactory; however, this is no longer true. Although there are still a few who claim better response and a truer snare drum sound is produced by playing on the calfskin heads, most educators and professional musicians now utilize the plastic heads. The following is a table listing comparative advantages of plastic heads over the calfskin heads:

Calfskin	*Plastic*
1. Subject to great variation in tension (and sound) by changes in the relative humidity.	1. Not affected by changes in relative humidity.
2. Subject to breakage through rapid changes in weather, puncture with drumsticks.	2. Less breakage, but care must be taken when mounting head. A rough edge on the drum shell may start a tear when tension is applied.
3. Longevity limited, as heads lose resiliency. Texture changes cause loss of responsiveness eventually.	3. Greater longevity, little change in resiliency with continued use.
4. Surface smooth and fairly hard textured when fresh, but becomes rough. Brushes rough up and eventually pierce head.	4. Surface texture very hard, and continued playing does not roughen head.
5. Considerable variation in uniformity from head to head.	5. Controlled uniformity in heads made by each manufacturer.
6. Stick response good when head is tuned properly and weather conditions optimum. Response poor in damp weather.	6. Stick response satisfactory. A harder "feel" to head is noted when first switching from calfskin head. Response same under all conditions.

In summary, the author recommends plastic heads for school use on the basis of their practicality and cost, which outweigh any slight disadvantage in tone quality.

The batter (top) heads for snare drums are thicker than the snare (bottom heads). Batter heads must be strong enough to withstand the impact of the sticks, while the snare head's thin gauge makes it extremely sensitive to vibration. It has been found that the hide of calves two to eight weeks old is best for snare drum batter heads. During the manufacturing process the skin is stretched uniformly from all sides until it turns white. This tends to make it stronger, but takes away some of the natural elasticity. Skins to be used for snare heads are taken from unborn calves. These transparent hides are called "slunk" skins. They are extremely elastic and sensitive to vibration. They are not stretched white, but used in their original clear, semitransparent state.

For the sake of natural appearance, plastic heads are manufactured to resemble calfskin. The batter heads are milky white in color and the snare heads transparent. The composition and gauge of the plastic snare and batter heads conform to the qualities found in the skin heads.

When purchasing drumheads, either calfskin or plastic, measure the diameter *inside* the rim. It is impractical for the player or instructor to mount drumheads on the flesh hoops. The time and skill required to mount drumheads is considerable, so it is well worth the extra dollar to buy the heads already mounted.

TENSION AND TUNING

Single and double tension are terms referring to the arrangement of tuning rods on drums. In single tension drums both heads are affected when a single rod is turned due to its having claw hooks over both snare and batter counterhoops (rims). Such an arrangement is used only on the lower priced drums and is not recommended because it is not then possible to make the necessary adjustment of each head independently. Double tension drums have a separate tension casing attached to the shell for each tuning rod. This arrangement provides for independent tuning at each tuning point on both the snare and batter heads.

The snare drumheads can be tuned in the following sequence of steps, beginning with the mounting of the head on the drum:

1. Loosen the tuning rods until they can be pulled out.
2. Remove counterhoop and the head to be replaced.
3. Wipe off dust and dirt accumulated around edge of shell; make sure shell is smooth and completely free from rough spots.
4. Fit new head over shell, pressing flesh hoop down as far as it will go.
5. Remount and align counterhoop.
6. Replace tuning rods and screw them down by hand until they are snug and height of counterhoop is even all the way around.
7. Using the drum key, give each rod one or two half-turns. Tune opposite, not adjacent, rods. Repeat process until head is fairly tight.

8. Test for sound with drumstick. Check evenness of counterhoop. Apply more tension if needed.

9. Final tuning of batter head should result in a head which can be depressed *only slightly* by pressing the thumb down in the center of the head.

10. In replacing and tuning the snare head it will be necessary to remove the snares. The procedure is then the same as for the batter head. The thumb should depress the head *slightly* more than for the batter head.

The most common tuning fault among school players is failure to tighten snare drumheads enough. Loose heads will not produce the typical snare drum sound. Remember the "rule of thumb"— the batter head should be depressable only very slightly; the snare head *almost* as tight.

It is best to change calfskin heads and set the tuning when the air is dry. If too much tension is applied when the air is moist a sudden change to dry weather may break the head. Once tuned carefully in dry weather, the snare drumheads should not be changed. It is *not* a good idea to tighten and loosen snare drums each time they are used. Of course, if the drum must be played on a very humid day, it will be necessary to increase the tension by turning *each rod* an *equal* amount. Immediately after use on such a day, loosen the head by the same number of half turns used to tighten it before storing. Otherwise, a broken drumhead is likely to result when the humidity dips. Plastic heads once set will need only a very occasional increase in tension to compensate for a slight amount of stretching. Calfskin heads will require more attention.

SNARE DRUMSTICKS

Snare drumsticks should be selected for the particular drum with which they are to be used. In general, a shallow dance band type drum will respond best with comparatively light sticks and a deep field drum requires heavy sticks to bring out its best tones. Manufacturers have a rough system of classifying sticks by number and letter. Unfortunately leading manufacturers of sticks have never standardized the weights, lengths and shapes of sticks by uniform letter-number designations. Ludwig and Slingerland use the letters *A* for so-called orchestra sticks, *B* for band, and *S* for street (drum corps). Gretsch uses *D* for dance band sticks, *C* for concert (orchestra or band)

RECOMMENDED MODELS

Recommended snare drums for school use are summarized in the following table:

School Level	Types	Tension	Dimensions	Heads	Snares
Elementary	Concert or	Double	6½" x 14"	Plastic	Wire
	Dance	Double	5" x 14"	Plastic	Wire
	Field	Single	10" x 14"	Plastic	Wire
Junior High	Concert	Double	6½" x 14"	Plastic	Wire-gut
	Dance	Double	5½" x 14"	Plastic	Wire
	Field	Double	10" x 14"	Plastic	Wire-gut
High School	Concert	Double	8" x 15"	Plastic or Skin	Wire-gut 18 strand
	Dance	Double	5½" x 14"	Plastic	Wire
	Field	Double	12" x 15"	Plastic	Wire-gut
College-University	Concert	Double	8" x 15"	Plastic or Skin	Wire-gut 18 strand
	Dance	Double	5½" x 14"	Plastic	Wire
	Field	Double	12" x 16"	Plastic	Wire-gut

and *P* for parade. The numbering is even more confusing as variables of shape, weight, and length are incorporated in the numbers assigned. The purchaser must acquaint himself with several of the more useful models, and use these as points of reference if further experimentation is needed.

Most drumsticks are made from straight grained white hickory wood. Rosewood sticks were once somewhat popular, but are rarely seen now. A leading maker of plastic drumheads now markets plastic drumsticks, but their weight, balance and "feel" do not approximate hickory sticks. Eventually the plastic drumstick may reach a point of development where it will gain acceptance by professionals, but as of the date of writing they cannot be endorsed. Sticks with nylon tips are available for approximately 50¢ extra per pair. These tips do have the advantages of being more durable, not chipping, and creating fewer nicks in drum heads.

PARTS OF THE INSTRUMENT

The diagram following illustrates the parts of the snare drum.

Figure 3.4. Parts of the Snare Drum.

Drum Type	Dimensions	Use	Sticks
Field	10″ x 14″	Marching band Concert band	Ludwig 2B Slingerland 2A
Field	12″ x 15″	Drum corps or marching band Concert band	Ludwig 2S Slingerland 2B
Concert	6½″ x 14″	Orchestra Concert band	Slingerland 2A Leedy 20
Concert	8″ x 15″	Orchestra Concert band	Ludwig 5B Leedy 20
Dance	6½″ x 14″	Dance band	Slingerland "Deems Model"
Dance	5″ x 14″	Dance band or jazz combo	Slingerland 5A

Drumsticks should be personally selected, never ordered by mail. It is necessary to test each stick for straightness, which is easily done by rolling it along a smooth surface such as a glass countertop. Each pair should be matched for weight and balance, either by holding one in each hand or by actually weighing them on the small scale which many dealers have for the purpose.

It is not necessary for beginning students to buy a pair of the very heavy "practice" sticks. A better plan is to select a medium weight all-purpose stick that will be strong enough to use on the practice pad and will also be fairly well matched to the drum.

The recommended sticks for beginning elementary school children with very small hands are Slingerland 6A, Ludwig 2A, 4A. For all other beginning students the Slingerland 2A is recommended.

Sticks for use with representative sizes of drums and for particular styles of music are suggested in the above table:

Figure 3.5. Parts of the Snare Drumstick.

HOLDING THE STICKS

Until recent years, there was considered to be one correct way of holding snare drum sticks, that being the traditional grip. Now, there is a rather large group of percussionists advocating the use of the "matched grip"—that is, a grip whereby both hands grasp the sticks in a like manner using the right hand grip of the traditional method as a model for both hands. This "newer" method (it is really not a new method since it has been experimented with for some time. It was never officially recognized as a correct method of holding the sticks.) has definite advantages and should be considered seriously by all modern day percussionists. First of all, it alleviates the awkward and unnatural left hand grip and makes much more sense to the beginning student. Secondly, it facilitates the learning of the other percussion instruments since the matched grip for snare drum is quite akin to grips used with the mallet instruments and timpani.

The traditional grip has the obvious advantage over the matched grip in marching organizations which do not utilize the "hi-steppers." After all, this is why the traditional grip developed as it did. The snare drum was first a martial instrument. When it was introduced into the concert hall, its basic technique accompanied it there, including the slant of the drum, the traditional grip, and the rudimental approach to playing. The traditional grip, also, has some advantages when performing on a set.

Since, without a doubt, the traditional method will continue to be used and since the matched grip method utilizes, basically, the right hand technique of the traditional approach for both hands, it is felt best to proceed with a detailed discussion of the traditional grip.

Right Hand

The R stick is grasped in a rather natural manner, as one would grasp any stick of wood if it were handed to him, at a point 1/3 of the distance up from the butt end of the stick. The thumb nail should fall along the L side of the stick and point straight toward the tip. The other point of contact to form the R fulcrum is the flesh of the first joint of the R forefinger. See Figures 3.6 and 3.7.

Figure 3.7. Bottom View, R.

Figure 3.6. Top View, R.

The three remaining R fingers are curled loosely around the stick, maintaining always a *light* contact with the upper shaft of the stick. They do not tighten to a genuine grip, as this would prevent the stick's natural rebound. The butt end of the stick will protrude slightly from the right side of the wrist, in order to avoid its hitting the underwrist. See Figure 3.7. In correct *ready* position the R wrist is *flat across the top.* The action of the wrist is forward and back. As an aid in establishing a correct concept of the R wrist action, ask the student to imagine that he is casting a fly rod as far as possible out into the water. He will recall that a whip-like action produces the desired result. Another useful teaching device is to simulate the action of cracking a whip. The entire

arm, wrist and hand are involved. These or similar calisthenic exercises should be practiced in mid-air before proceeding to the practice of the R stroke on the pad or drum.

Left Hand

The L handhold and wrist action are not as "natural" as those of the R. It is recommended that the following sequence of steps be used when introducing the L handhold. The Sequence of figures illustrates each concept. Each should be studied carefully.

Step One

Extend the L arm full length in front of the body, fingers and thumb forming a vertical plane with the floor, fingers together. See Figure 3.8.

Figure 3.8

Step Two

Grasp the stick by the tip with the right hand and insert it at the balancing point 1/3 the distance up from the butt end, between the thumb and the side of the palm, as far down into the webby crease as possible. Hold firmly at right angles to the palm. See Figure 3.9.

Figure 3.11

Figure 3.9

Figure 3.12

Step Three

The L wrist rotates in its action. Its *ready* position is approximately vertical. Start from the position shown in step two and rotate the wrist, *slowly at first,* around as far in either direction as the wrist will turn. Take care to hold the stick snugly enough to prevent its falling down to a position parallel with the palm. It must be maintained at right angles to the L wrist. The value of this calisthenic lies in forcing the wrist to turn all the way in either direction. The action is similar to that used in turning a doorknob. The rotary action should be practiced in mid-air before the actual L handhold is introduced. See Figures 3.10, 3.11, and 3.12.

Step Four

With the stick still held securely in the web between thumb and palm, turn the ring and little fingers under until they almost reach the palm. These two fingers serve as a bouncing pad for the **L** stick. See Figure 3.13.

Figure 3.10

Figure 3.13

Step Five

Shift the direction of the thumb to a position pointing *down* the shaft toward the stick tip. It will bend at the joint slightly and may contact the top of the shaft for all or most of its length. See Figure 3.14.

Figure 3.14

Step Six

Curl the index and middle fingers *loosely* around the stick to maintain a *very light* contact with the top of the shaft when in *ready* position. (See Figure 3.15.) These fingers must give way, or open up, when the stick travels its normal course in making the full arm stroke. (See Figure 3.16.) There is a slight contact of the index finger at its first joint with the tip of the thumb, which will have to "break" on the back swing of the full stroke.

Figure 3.15

Figure 3.16

The principle danger in the L is that the stick will not be held firmly at its fulcrum by the thumb. *Never* should there be any space between the stick and the webby part of the thumb joint. Students should be cautioned "never to see light" between the L stick and the base of the thumb joint.

Note: No concession is made to handedness in percussion technique. Left-handed students should hold the sticks in the same manner as those who are right-handed. This is logical, since both hands perform an equal service. Another factor is the impracticality of drumming left-handed in the marching band, at the drum set, or in any situation where players rotate on a certain set of instruments.

List of Common Faults—R and L Handholds

1. Stick not held at balancing point (1/3 distance from butt end).
2. R thumb pointing down instead of straight along shaft.
3. Forming R grip with second instead of index finger.
4. R wrist not flat but tilted over to the right.
5. L wrist not vertical but tilted over to the left.
6. L stick not held firmly enough at fulcrum.
7. Index and second fingers of L hand pressing down on stick shaft.
8. L wrist bent out away from body instead of extending straight from forearm.

PLAYING POSITION

Concert Snare Drum

The playing position for the concert snare drum is shown in Figure 3.17.

Figure 3.17. Playing Position, Concert Snare Drum.

The drum is set on the stand by the following procedure:

Figure 3.18

1. Fit two sections of stand together, then raise top section to a position 8″ to 10″ below player's beltline. Set height adjustment screw. See Figure 3.18.
2. Spread three arms of stand to their holding positions. Pull adjustable arm out to maximum length. See Figure 3.19.
3. Turn stand so that the two nonadjustable arms are to the right, the adjustable arm pointing toward the player's left. Tighten angle adjustment screw. See Figure 3.20.
4. Place drum on stand with the snare throw-off lever *to the left,* next to, but not on, the section of the arm that bends upward. See Figure 3.21.

Figure 3.19

Figure 3.20

5. Push adjustable arm in until it grasps drum securely, then tighten set screw. See Figure 3.22.

Figure 3.21

6. Adjust angle of drum so that it tilts slightly toward the right. See Figure 3.23.

Figure 3.23

The instructor should demonstrate the foregoing procedure and then insist that these steps be faithfully adhered to whenever a drum is set on a stand. Students are often careless in this matter and many broken drumheads, cracked drum shells, and bent wire snares occur as a result.

Figure 3.22

Figure 3.24. Concert Snare Drum Rest Position.

The height and slant of the concert snare drum may show a slight variation according to player preference, but a good rule is to have the drum 2 to 4 inches below belt height, and the right side about an inch lower than the left side. See Figure 3.17 for a good playing position. The music rack should be raised to the player's chest height.

Note: The snare drummer in the concert band and orchestra *always* stands. The seated position for the dance band drummer will be dealt with in a later chapter.

Rest Position

Rest position is shown in Figure 3.24.

Rest position should be assumed during all rests of more than a measure or two duration. During tacet portions of the music the snare drummer should be seated.

Field Drum

Playing position for the field drum is shown in Figure 3.25.

Figure 3.26

Figure 3.25. Field Drum Playing Position.

2. Grasp the small hook with the left hand, bring it around to the front and fasten it through the eyelet.

Figure 3.27

The steps for slinging the field drum are:
1. Place sling over right shoulder with latch in front.

3. Adjust the height by means of the adjusting device until the latch is about 2″ below belt height.

Figure 3.28

4. Pick up the drum with the left hand and snap the latch to the carrying hook.

Figure 3.29

The field drum will hang at a pronounced slant over the left leg.

Rest position for the field drum is similar to that for the concert drum. During tacet portions of the music the drum may be unslung quietly and the player may be seated. Music racks should be chest high.

Check List for Mounting Drum and Playing Positions

1. Is drum too high? Too low?
2. Is angle of tilt correct?
3. Is snare throw-off to the player's left?
4. Are the arms of drum stand correctly spaced?
5. Is player standing at right angle to direction of drum's tilt?
6. Is player erect and alert?
7. Does player assume proper rest position during rests?

List of Common Faults

1. Arms of snare drum stand bent, causing snares to catch on set-screw.
2. Arms of stand not spread properly.
3. Adjustable arm pointing right instead of left.
4. Snare throw-off not to player's left.
5. Drum too low.
6. Drum tilted too low on the right side.
7. Field drum sling not attached to drum properly.
8. "Slouching."
9. Failure to adopt proper rest position.

PLAYING SPOT

The playing spot on the batter head of the snare drum is dependent on the sound desired. For maximum resonance the drum should be struck slightly off center. The exact center is a nodal point in the vibrational pattern of the drumhead. Blows struck at dead center are actually dead sounding. Consequently when an extremely dry tone is desired, drummers play at the center of the head. For very soft notes the portions of the head near the rim are used. In general, the softer notes are played near the edges and louder tones nearer the center. Both sticks do not have to strike within the area of a 25-cent piece, as is often said. So long as they remain equidistant from the rims they will produce like sounds. This separation of sticks allows the arms to hang at a uniform and comfortable angle, whereas if both sticks were kept close to one another in moving toward the rim, one of the player's arms would be drawn out of its natural relaxed position.

Figures 3.30, 3.31, and 3.32 show playing spots for loud, moderately loud, and soft tones. Notice the manner in which the sticks are separated.

Figure 3.30. Snare drum playing spot, loud tone.

Figure 3.32. Snare drum playing spot, soft tone.

Figure 3.31. Snare drum playing spot, moderately loud tone.

The two sticks are held in playing position so that they form a right angle. Note that this angle is maintained whether the stick tips are close together or widely separated.

The beginning student should avoid extremes and use playing spots about one or two inches off center.

Even while practicing on the pad it is recommended that the sticks be separated by at least 1½″ or 2″.

Common Faults

1. Less than a 45° angle between sticks.
2. One stick nearer the rim than the other, producing unlike tones.
3. Colliding stick tips, caused by attempting to play within too small an area.
4. Playing at or near center in soft passages.
5. Not varying the playing spots with varying dynamic levels.

STICKING

Stickwork, sometimes called *sticking* refers to the choices of right or left sticks within rhythm figures. Thus, for the rhythm figure

the stickwork designation is RRLRL. In beginning drum music the stickwork is usually given for each note. In actual scores stickwork indications are seldom given. An important part of a player's training is the development of a system of sticking which can be applied almost automatically in reading any rhythm figure. Much attention must be given to good stickwork habit formation from the outset, otherwise haphazard or incorrect sticking will eventually inhibit good sight reading, and hamper technique. An analogous situation would result if the pianist were unsure of his scale fingerings. Stickwork is one aspect of a percussionist's performance skill which should require little, if any, conscious effort. In order to achieve this semiautomatic level it is necessary to lay a firm foundation of consciously recognized correct responses from the very first lesson.

There are two generally used systems of stickwork. One might be termed the *strict alternation system* and the other the *right-lead system.*

According to the *alternation system* successive notes, no matter what their duration or grouping, are played from hand-to-hand. "Hand-to-hand" is drummer's parlance for strict alternation. Showing no particular preference for starting hand, once begun the music is played with the sticks "as they come." The previously mentioned rhythm figure

might be played either RLRLR or LRLRL.

The *right-lead system* of stickwork, as its name implies, uses the R as the starting hand for figures commencing on a strong beat. First beats in each measure (with certain exceptions in triple meter), and subsequent strong beats are played by the R. The L is used for weak beats and for notes of less than one unit's duration. Pick-ups with one or three notes start with a L, two or four-note pick-ups begin with a R. Long rolls and many of the short rolls begin and end with a R. The following examples of common measures of snare drum music will serve to illustrate the application of the right-lead system of stickwork: (Parentheses show where the sticking is optional)

$\frac{4}{4}$ Quarter Notes and Rests

$\frac{4}{4}$ Quarter Notes and Rests

*Afterbeat measure

$\frac{4}{4}$ Quarter and Eighth Notes and Rests

Note: All dactylic figures played RRL.

Two-quarter and C measures corresponding to the foregoing 4/4 measures would follow the same stick-work indications. Asterisks indicate exceptions, as in the afterbeat measure. The principal reason that alternate sticks are used in playing this very typical snare drum rhythm is that such a figure usually occurs in chains of many repeated measures. It would be somewhat ridiculous to play 8, 16, or more measures with only one hand, hence the practice of alternating afterbeats has become standardized:

$\frac{3}{4}$ Quarter Notes and Rests

S. D. waltz rhythm always played as in example 2.

$\frac{3}{4}$ Quarter and Eighth Notes and Rests

$\frac{6}{8}$ Most Common Figures

also written

The author recommends the right-lead system in preference to the alternate sticking system for the following reasons:

1. It is used by the majority of fine percussionists.
2. Most of the best snare drum instruction methods employ it.
3. It is systematic and hence preferable to haphazard stick choice.
4. It facilitates sight reading because idiomatic figures, once learned, are always played the same way.
5. In reading unusual or complex figures the player has a working principle to guide choice of sticks.
6. It is advantageous in working at the drum set, where the R is basically concerned with the principally accented beats (cymbal notes, etc.) and the L is associated with the afterbeats.

7. A musically valid association is established between the R (strong beats, natural accents, first beats) and the L (pick-up notes, weak beats, fractional parts of beats, artificial accents, as in syncopation). Stickwork thus corresponds to the general principle of bowing a string instrument, wherein the first beat is usually played down bow, the next (weak) beat with an up bow. The R stick may be likened to the down bow, the L to the up bow.

Several points in connection with stickwork should be carefully noted. First, the addition of grace note combinations (called flams, drags, and ruffs in drummer's parlance) does *not* affect the basic sticking arrangement. For example,

$$\begin{array}{c}
\text{\musical phrase} \\
\text{L R L R R L R L} \quad \text{and} \quad \text{LL R L R RR L R L}
\end{array}$$

Second, it is very important for the student to learn and consistently apply the proper stickwork for the idiomatic rhythm figures. Stated simply—always play like measures with the same sticking.

Third, care must be taken when using some of the beginning band and orchestra methods to see that the faulty stick indications are corrected. The authors of these books seem to have proceeded on the false assumption that snare drum stickwork is simply a matter of starting at the first note with either a R or L and taking turns with the sticks until the final note is reached. Particularly confusing to the student are those books which give two sets of stickings for every exercise. A second fallacy which seems to have gained currency among instrumental class method writers is that the L is the weak hand, and by starting everything with the L it will somehow gain strength. There exists no justification for this practice, any more than could the teaching of bowings exactly opposite to those actually used be justified for the beginning student on the theory that up bows are more difficult than down bows and need special emphasis. Finally, it should be noted that this system requires greater concentration from the beginning student, but ultimately, through its teaching of consistency and uniformity, it frees the student to direct his concentrative efforts toward all the other musical problems.

THE STROKE

The most fundamental of all drum techniques is the full arm stroke. In preparation for making the stroke, hold the stick tips up about 1½″ above the practice pad. This is the starting point for all drum strokes and is called *ready position*. The full arm stroke on the drum is a three phase action: backswing; downswing; rebound (follow through). The sequence of figures illustrates the steps in making a R stroke.

Figure 3.33. Ready position.

On the backswing, the wrist initiates the action by humping up, leaving the tip of the stick lagging somewhat behind.

Figure 3.34. Wrist starts the action.

Lift arm until elbow is nearly shoulder high.

After impact, the stick's natural rebound then settles back to ready position and the R stroke is completed.

Figure 3.35. Lift arm.

Figure 3.37. Rebound.

The wrist starts down first, stick tip lags behind. Motion accelerates, reaching maximum velocity as stick strikes drumhead.

Figure 3.36. Start of downswing.

A useful teaching device is to have the student imagine that the stick tips are heavily weighted. This will aid in achieving a whip-like action of the arm, wrist and hand.

Common error. In practicing a series of R strokes, the stick is not allowed to settle back to ready position (1½″ above drumhead) before making the next stroke. Take much time between strokes. Practice a series of R strokes.

The L stroke is similar to the R except for the hand-hold and rotating wrist motion. Most students will find their first attempt to execute the L stroke clumsy and unsatisfactory. They will need encouragement and assurance that everyone has trouble with this awkward motion at first, but with daily practice it will soon seem as natural as the R. The sequence of Figures 3.38-3.42 illustrates the steps in making a L stroke.

On the backswing, the left wrist rotates first to the right slightly, leaving the tip of the stick lagging somewhat behind.

Lift arm until hand is nearly shoulder high.

Figure 3.38.   Ready position.

Figure 3.40.   Lift arm.

Figure 3.39.   Backswing.

Figure 3.41.   Wrist starts downswing.

Wrist rotates at top of backswing to the left, and initiates the downswing by a sudden rotation to the right.

After impact, stick's natural rebound then settles back to ready position and the L stroke is completed.

The index finger and thumb contact breaks at the top of the backswing, closing again during the rebound. The rotating motion of the wrist is the key to a good L stroke.

Practice a series of L strokes slowly.

When both the R and L strokes have been practiced independently, begin their slow alternation, R then L. This alternation of full arm strokes is the foundation of drum technique. Space the strokes about two seconds apart. Check between each stroke for ways to improve. As in golf, one should take plenty of time between practice shots in order to think of all factors and to correct mistakes. A helpful aid in

Figure 3.42. Rebound.

Figure 3.43. Ready position.

eliminating useless side motions of the sticks is to think of a track, or a slot, about 2″ or 3″ wide, within which each stick must execute its backswing and downswing.

Common Faults—R and L Strokes

1. Arm and wrist too rigid.

2. Waste motion caused by sticks "looping" outside the imaginary track.

3. Sticks not rebounding naturally.

4. Failure to allow sticks to settle back to ready position after rebound.

5. Failure to maintain correct grip on sticks.

6. Students' reluctance to exaggerate the arm motion. It should be pointed out to the student that this is an exaggeration (lifting elbow to shoulder level) and except in rare instances would the arms be raised to this level, examples being *sfz* attacks and performance with a marching band.

THE TAP

The tap is a single blow used to produce moderately light sounds on the snare drum. It differs from the stroke in that it is a *wrist* action, and does not involve the arms to any appreciable extent. A large percentage of snare drum music is played using only al-

ternated taps, the strokes being reserved for very heavy sounds and accents. Figures 3.43-3.45 illustrate the steps in making a R tap.

Starting from ready position, snap the wrist sharply, as in the stroke, but without raising the arm. This will produce a rather loud tap.

Figure 3.44. Start of wrist action.

The arc travelled by the stick tip will be approximately 12" to 14". Play a series of R taps slowly, keeping stick arc and volume equal for all notes.

Consequently, the arc of the stick tip will not usually be as regular as it should be, either in its length or straightness.

Figure 3.45. Start of downswing, R tap.

Figure 3.47. Start of downswing, L tap.

Figures 3.46-3.48 illustrate the steps in making a L tap.

To produce the same sound with the L stick, use the same 12" to 14" arc. Control is more difficult here, as the L handhold may still be in its awkward stage.

Figure 3.46. Ready position, L tap.

Figure 3.48. Rebound, L tap.

Students will need to be reminded frequently of the imaginary track within which each stick is to travel. Check also on the wrist actions. Remember— R wrist moves forward and back, L wrist rotates.

As in all percussion stroking, the taps require a whip-like stick motion with a natural rebound and follow through. Even though these motions will be smaller than those used in the full arm stroke, they are nonetheless necessary in order to avoid a stiff-wristed, crushed sound. Always remember that any percussion blow must get-on-and-get-off the struck surface to produce a good tone.

Practice a series of taps, R and L, slowly.

When the loud taps (12 to 14 inch stick arcs) can be done fairly well, shorten the arcs in order to produce a softer tone. Less wrist motion will be required to do this, but more control is necessary and is obtained through the fine muscle and nerve coordination of the hands and fingers. The stick arc for *p* volume is about 2 inches.

Common Faults—R and L Taps

1. Wrist too rigid.
2. Use of arm motion—only wrist motion is required.
3. Lack of stick control which causes buzz or unwanted sounds.
4. Failure to maintain correct grip on sticks.
5. Index finger of left hand failing to break contact with thumb, consequently preventing a correct arc to be traversed by the stick.

THE LONG ROLL

There are two basic ways of producing a sustained tone on percussion instruments. These are the *single stroke roll*, which is used on the timpani, bass drum, xylophone, marimba, bells, suspended cymbal, timbales, and occasionally the snare drum, and the *double stroke roll* which is the usual method of producing a long tone on the snare drum. The single stroke roll is made by rapidly alternating R and L blows on the playing surface of the instrument. The double stroke roll consists of rapidly alternating double strokes, RRLL etc., in which the first of each pair is a tap and the second a bounce. Since we are here dealing with snare drum techniques, only the double stroke roll will be considered in the following discussion.

Before introducing the stepwise procedures useful in teaching the snare drum roll, some general remarks should be given to clarify commonly used terminology and to enable the reader to gain an insight into the development of the roll as it is used in various styles of modern drumming. It often comes as somewhat of a surprise to nonpercussion playing laymen, musicians, and teachers to learn that today's all-around snare drummer actually uses an assortment of rolls which vary in duration, texture (degree of openness) and timbre. Factors which influence the type of roll are size of drum, style of music, volume desired, weight of sticks, thickness of drumhead, response of drum, and personal tastes.

The original sustaining tone of the military drum was very likely what we would now call an "open" roll, i.e., each individual tap-and-bounce sound could be distinguished by the ear. Before the introduction of the snare drum into the concert hall it was associated mainly with marching music, and this usage demanded loud, open rolls whose texture (timing of taps and bounces) conformed to the marching cadence. Wrist alternations were synchronized with the footfalls of the marching drummer's feet.

With the advent of smaller and more responsive drums a change in the roll technique gradually evolved. The rolls became more closed and less "rhythmic," i.e., wrist motions were not synchronized with the pulse of the beat.

Although there is no proof, it is likely that the first drummers to use what is now called the "buzz" roll were the early dance and vaudeville drummers around the turn of the last century. In this type of roll individual sounds are indistinguishable and the ideal is a continuous tone, very smooth in texture. It has been likened to the tearing of silk cloth. In the buzz roll more than two sounds are produced per wrist action.

Percussion instructors are divided into two rather distinct camps on the matter of how to teach the roll. One group sticks by the traditional approach of RRLL strokes *gradually* increased in speed through the taps on into the tap-and-bounce of the open roll, and finally attaining the speed of the closed roll. In this approach the student may not go at any rate faster than perfect evenness of timing and volume permit. The crucial point in the development of the roll using the traditional approach is the so-called "break" or "gear-shifting" point, when the acceleration rate becomes too fast to continue one sound per wrist motion and two-sounds-per-wrist-motion (tap and bounce) take over.

In the newer approach the student is not forced to spend weeks and months on roll development, but is provided with a double stroke roll at the outset, which he then perfects through practice until it becomes as controlled as that roll developed by the traditional method.

Good rolls have been developed by both methods. Generally the private teacher working with an able student will subscribe to the first method. The school instructor working with groups of students in a beginning band, orchestra or percussion class will find the second method most useful. Both methods of teaching the roll are outlined in this *Guide*. Following the teaching outlines there is a table summarizing advantages and disadvantages of each.

Steps in Learning the Roll, Traditional Method

The long roll is produced by alternating double strokes, RRLL etc. At first it should be played wide open, using two large strokes with each hand. It will be some weeks or months before the alternations can be speeded up (and stick arc cut down) through the taps, and on down into the open roll which is produced by a tap-and-bounce. At first this will not sound anything like a roll. Impatient students must be impressed with the fact that development of a fine roll is a long, continuous process. The criteria for determining the rapidity of alternations are 1. evenness and 2. equality of volume.

Practice the slow RRLL with no accented or predominant sounds. Equal stick arcs will help to maintain equal sounds. At beginning stages it is best to maintain a steady tempo. After the RRLL pattern has become fairly automatic, introduce the idea of gradual acceleration. Remind students that it is desirable to accelerate as much as possible *so long as perfect evenness of time and volume are maintained.* It is suggested that ten minutes of a 30 minute daily practice period be devoted to roll practice.

Speed up the alternation of the taps until reaching a point where it becomes necessary to "double up" and execute the RRLL by means of one tap followed by one bounce of the same stick. Now, instead of two wrist motions, only one is needed for each pair of sounds. This "shifting of gears" makes the closed roll possible. It is this shift from single taps to tap-and-bounce which is a hurdle requiring much practice and perseverance to surmount. To make the acceleration of sound up to, through, and on beyond this shift without disturbing the gradations of acceleration is the goal of practice.

If real control has been achieved, the reverse process, closed-to-open will be easily executed. Rudimental drum contests require the roll be demonstrated in this fashion: open-to-close-to-open.

Steps in Learning the Roll, Newer Method

Beginning with the R alone, make a tap using about a 14" arc. Next let the tap's natural rebound strike the pad (or drumhead) *once*. This will sound as "da-da" and consists of one tap plus one bounce, made with a single motion of the wrist. It will require

considerable practice to achieve a single bounce sound which is controlled and is as loud as the tap which it follows.

When the R "da-da" can be done consistently, repeat the procedure with the L alone. Remember— try to make the bounce sound equal to the tap in each pair. Take plenty of time between practice tries. A slight downward pressure of fingers and hand on the top of the stick controls the rebound in order to get just *one* bounce.

When enough control is achieved and two fairly equal sounds are being consistently played with each hand, try synchronizing the wrist alternations to produce a continuous flow, RRLLRRLL, etc. Do not allow any gaps in the flow, even if all bounces are not sounding. There should never be any "holes" in the roll, even at this stage. A very useful teaching device to aid the student in gaining the right concept of wrist alternation speed is for the instructor to stand behind the student and grasp his hands and manipulate the student's wrists at the rate required for the open roll. See Figure 3.49.

Figure 3.49. Teacher guiding student's hands and wrists.

The closed roll is made by lowering the stick arcs and speeding up the wrist alternations.

A useful concept in teaching the roll by the newer method is "let the sticks do the work." The idea is to utilize the energy of the rebounding stick in making the controlled bounce. Timing is all-important. Diligent practice is required to perfect the long roll no matter how it is taught.

Long Roll Taught By

Traditional Method

Cannot be used in playing drum music until perfected.

Best adapted for individual study.

Takes much patience; frustration occurs in conquering "the break."

Required in rudimental demonstrations.

For those who wish to pursue the subject of the so-called buzz roll, an excellent article by George Lawrence Stone appears in his column in the January, 1961, issue of the *International Musician*, titled "Two Beat Roll vs. the Buzz."

Common Faults—The Long Roll

1. Failure to maintain an even rate of acceleration in passing over the "break" (traditional approach).
2. Making more than one bounce sound following each tap (newer approach).
3. Failure to make the bounce sound equal to the tap.
4. Gaps in the long roll due to poor timing of wrist alternations.
5. Pressing or crushing sticks down into drumhead, resulting in scratchy texture of roll.
6. Stiffness of wrist action.
7. Inconsistent volume level between the two hands. The tendency is for one hand to predominate.

Note—for rolls of soft and medium volumes only finger, hand and wrist actions are required. In loud playing, the forearms, upper arms and shoulders are brought into play.

Notation of rolls is treated in a later section of this chapter under *Notation of Snare Drum Music.*

A useful device for aiding the intermediate or advanced snare drummer to improve his long roll is to practice pulsating in both binary and ternary patterns. The following diagrams illustrate this concept.

Newer Method

Can be used when reading introduced, although not yet perfected.

Best adapted for class study.

Sounds like a roll from the start. The challenge is to smooth it up, control degree of openness.

Traditional approach, open-to-closed-to-open would have to be developed later to demonstrate long roll "rudimentally."

For a detailed treatment of roll texture, the reader is referred to pages 11-13 of *Beginning Snare Drum Method* by Paul Price, published by Morris.

THE SHORT ROLLS

The three short or stroke rolls most commonly used in snare drumming are the 5, 7 and 9 stroke rolls. They may be conceived as segments of the long roll, and their introduction should be delayed until the student has developed a fairly smooth and well controlled long roll. Idiomatically the short rolls are used in rudimental and orchestral snare drumming when notes of short value are indicated as rolls. The choice of stroke roll to be used in each case is governed primarily by the tempo of the music and secondarily by the style (rudimental, orchestral, jazz, etc.). In most rudimentally oriented instruction books and in rudimental solo literature, small numerals are often placed over rolled notes to indicate which of the short rolls is to be used.

In all other music the choice of stroke roll is left to the performer.

More often than not the short rolls will be found to commence on weak beats, or fractional parts of a beat, and end with their final tap on a strong beat. Pick-ups to marching cadences are a good example.

In such weak-tied-to-strong-beat rolls the accent falls on the final single tap of the roll. When short rolls commence on a strong beat they are accented on their starting note, and are called *accented 5, 7, or 9 stroke rolls*. In accented stroke rolls, no emphasis is placed on the final single tap which then serves merely to conclude the alternate double strokes.

Much confusion about stroke rolls would be dispelled if percussion teaching would emphasize the salient point that *the short roll is merely a segment of a long roll adjusted to fill a certain time-slot*. Needless time is often spent learning and practicing, out of any musical context, 10, 11, 13, 15, 17, even 21 stroke rolls. The experienced percussionist knows that when the notation calls for a roll on a note of short duration he will start and end his roll to coincide with the beat, and only in retrospect will he be able to say whether he has used a 5, 7, 9, or 17 stroke roll. Only when interpreting a traditional rudimental passage will the drummer need to be particularly conscious of the exact number of strokes in the short rolls.

Despite the above remarks, all percussion students should practice the most commonly used of the stroke rolls as a part of their early training. The 5, 7, and 9 stroke rolls are somewhat similar, but will be treated separately in the material which follows.

The 5 Stroke Rolls

The 5 stroke rolls consist of two groups of doubled notes and a final single tap.

The foregoing examples show the breakdown of the 5 stroke rolls, but are not intended to illustrate actual notation as it would be found in drum music.

The accent here is on the final note. Three wrist motions are required in the 5 stroke roll.

In an open 5 stroke roll, the ear can distinguish the 5 sounds, but when the roll is closed the meshing of the sounds blurs the individual taps and bounces. In fact, a very closed 5 stroke roll will be of the same texture as the previously mentioned buzz roll in which there is no proof that each stick actually sounds only twice. The buzz texture is adaptable to the short rolls whenever the performer wishes to produce a sound of very fine texture. In order to clarify a confusing point of terminology, it should be pointed out that the so-called "press roll" or "crush roll" is not identical to the buzz roll. The press or crush roll is made by pressing both sticks on the drumhead simultaneously and allowing them to buzz for an instant or two. This method of production does not conform to that of a true roll, but it is nonetheless useful in certain cases such as the following, where there is not time enough to execute a legitimate 5 stroke roll:

Dance and jazz drummers have pioneered in the use of the press roll, and have even developed a technique of producing a roll with a single stick. For a more detailed treatment of this subject refer to Chapter 9, *Dance Band Drumming*.

Five stroke rolls occuring in series are usually alternated, as:

A few examples of passages where the snare drummer would be likely to use a 5 stroke roll are:

The accented 5 stroke roll has the same number of sounds and requires the same number of wrist motions (3) as the 5 stroke roll just described. The difference in execution is that the accented 5 stroke roll has an accent at its beginning and none on its final single tap. The difference in usage is that the accented 5 stroke roll is used when the rolled note starts on a primarily accented beat, or when an artificial accent is indicated.

Examples are here given which illustrate situations calling for the accented 5 stroke roll.

Bright waltz tempo

Common Faults—5 Stroke Rolls

1. Among beginning students, the most common fault is failure to use 3 wrist motions to make the 5 stroke roll. Many students, if not checked carefully,

will play or

which does not produce an authentic 5 stroke roll.

2. Placing an accent at the end of the roll when roll falls on the beat, i.e., choosing a roll which does not make musical sense.

The 7 Stroke Rolls

The 7 stroke roll consists of three groups of doubled notes and a final single tap.

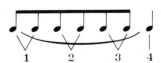

The foregoing examples show the breakdown of the 7 stroke rolls, but are not intended to illustrate the notation as it would be found in drum music.

The accent here is on the final note. Four wrist motions are required in the 7 stroke roll. Note carefully that the 7 stroke rolls do not end with the same stick with which they begin. In this they are unlike their companion short rolls, the 5 and 9.

As in the 5 stroke roll, when the 7 is played open all sounds will be distinguishable to the ear. Closed 7 stroke rolls will sound as a segment of the closed long roll. Remember that the degree of openness of any roll is dictated by tempo and style of the music. Seven stroke rolls occuring in a rudimental snare drum solo would be correctly played open.

Seven stroke rolls occuring in series are *not* alternated, for example:

Other examples of passages where the snare drummer would be likely to use 7 stroke rolls are:

Allegro

°When background beats (pulsations) are *ternary* a 7 stroke roll usually fits better than either a 5 or a 9. For this reason they are much used in 6/8, 9/8 and 12/8 time.

M.M. ♩ = 100 – 120

This figure illustrates the principle that tempo determines choice of stroke roll. Note same figure in sections on 5 and 9 stroke rolls.

If a 7 stroke roll starts on a strong or artificially accented beat, its accent is shifted from the final to the first note.

Accented 7 stroke rolls are not used as often as accented 5's or 9's. The following illustrate situations in which accented 7 stroke rolls might be used:

Vivo

Common Faults—7 Stroke Rolls

1. Poor timing of wrist alternation, which prevents roll from fitting nicely into its time-slot.

2. Accenting end of roll when roll commences on a strong beat.
3. Creating a feeling of decrescendo when performing accented 7 stroke rolls.

The 9 Stroke Rolls

The 9 stroke roll consists of four groups of doubled notes and a final single tap.

The foregoing examples show the breakdown of the 9 stroke rolls, but are not intended to illustrate actual notation as it would be found in drum music.

The accent here is on the final note. Five wrist motions are required in the 9 stroke roll.

In an open 9 stroke roll all nine sounds will be distinguishable to the ear. A closed 9 stroke roll will have the same fine-grained texture as any other closed roll. Like the 5, the 9 stroke roll will fit best into time-slots which are pulsated binarily. For example,

Nine stroke rolls are usually alternated when they occur in series:

A few examples of passages in which the snare drummer would be likely to employ 9 stroke rolls are:

M.M. ♩ = 60 – 80

Adagio

See same figure in sections on 5 and 7 stroke rolls, noting tempo difference.

The accented 9 stroke roll has the same number of sounds and requires the same number of wrist motions (5) as the 9 stroke roll just described. The difference in execution is the shift of the accent from the final to the first note of the roll. The difference in usage is that the accented 9 stroke roll is used when the rolled note starts on a primarily accented beat, or when an artificial accent is indicated.

Examples are here given which illustrate situations calling for the use of accented 9 stroke rolls.

Common Faults—9 Stroke Rolls

1. Poor timing of wrist alternations, which prevents roll from fitting nicely into its time-slot.
2. Accenting end of roll in a situation where roll commences on a strong beat.
3. Creating a feeling of decrescendo when performing accented 9 stroke rolls.

A more specialized treatment of the notation of the short rolls will be found in the section on *Notation of Snare Drum Music*.

For a description of the so-called 3 stroke roll the reader is referred to *Beginning Snare Drum Method* by Paul Price, published by Morris, pages 52-53. This same book treats in some detail the 11, 13, and 15 stroke rolls.

THE FLAM

In addition to single strokes and double strokes (rolls) a third class of drum techniques consists of the "thickening" sounds. Their function is to add duration and volume to the single stroke. They are used principally on natural or artificially accented beats.

The most often used thickening stroke is called the *flam*. The flam consists of a soft grace note played almost simultaneously with, but ahead of, a loud stroke. It is notated as it sounds; one "little" and one "big" sound.

The sound should approximate the one syllable word "flam"—it should *not* sound like the two-syllable "fa-lam."

Flams can be learned by following the sequence of steps here outlined:

1. Place both sticks in ready position (1½″ above drumhead).

Figure 3.50. Ready position, R or L flam.

Figure 3.51. R flam.

Figure 3.52. L flam.

2. Leaving the L where it is, raise the R and make a regular full arm stroke, dropping the L in *just ahead of the R* stroke. *Do not* allow the grace note stick to rise appreciably—it should drop and make a single quiet sound which serves to thicken the main note. Even in the open flam, the grace note should not precede the main note noticeably, and in the closed flam the two sounds are practically simultaneous, but never sounding exactly together. Practice a series of R flams slowly.

3. Reverse the roles of the two sticks to make a L flam. The R is now the grace note stick which drops in just ahead of the main L. Practice a series of L flams slowly.

4. When R and L flams can be executed satisfactorily, hand-to-hand flams should be practiced. A special trick is needed to get the natural rebound of the "big" stick down quickly to ready position in order for it to become the "little" stick for the alternate flam. Control the rebounding stick with a somewhat sudden tighter grip and thus force it to remain close to the drumhead. Do not force too stiffly, however, as some rebound is necessary and desirable. Drum parts seldom call for rapidly alternating flams, but they should be practiced hand-to-hand, at first open and then more closed. Practice a series of R and L flams, taking plenty of time between successive flams.

A useful teaching device is the encouragement of the student to "make the big stick bigger and the little stick littler." This will help to avoid those "faker's flams" which are neither R nor L because

both sticks are rising and falling in more or less equal arcs.

For loud flams use full arm strokes. When less volume is desired use lower stick arcs on the main notes. Very soft flams are made by using wrist taps on the main notes.

The grace note has no time value.

The grace note stick varies only slightly in its path for loud or soft flams.

Note: Stickwork remains the same when flams are called for as for single strokes, i.e., grace notes are not counted when determining sticking arrangement.

Common Faults—Flams

1. Grace note stick rises too much.
2. Grace note stick sounds too far ahead of main note. (*fa-lam* rather than *flam.*)
3. Both sticks striking head simultaneously defeating the purpose of the "flam" sound.
4. Grace note stick bounces, buzzes.
5. In alternating flams, both sticks rise equally.
6. Swinging arms from side to side.

THE DRAG

The second of the "thickening" strokes is called *the drag.* As in the case of the flam, the notation is a good visual symbol of the sound.

R Drag   L Drag

L L R   R R L

Two grace notes, made by the same stick, precede the main stroke. The grace notes drop in just ahead of the main note. In the open drag the three sounds are distinguishable to the ear, although felt by the player as a unit.

As in the flam, the "little" stick stays close to its ready position, and with a minimum of upward motion drops in just ahead of the main note. A controlled rebound follows the initial grace note tap. In hand-to-hand playing of the drags a tightening of the grip on the rebounding "big" stick is necessary because it must return very quickly to ready position in order to become the "little" stick for the alternate drag.

One problem that usually arises in the study of the drag is the tendency to fall into a rhythm pattern of ♫ | ♪ ♫ ♪ ♫ |etc. when practicing open drags. The drag itself has no rhythm, but sounds simply as a broad note. The soft grace notes supply the broadening sound *just barely* before the beat.

In the closed drag the two grace notes will be indistinguishable (as the individual taps and bounces of the finely closed roll) and will "drag" into the accented main note with a sound phonetically equivalent to "zzz-it."

Most students in learning to execute the drag need constant reminding that the stroke (main note) is louder and more important sounding than the grace notes which precede it. It must also land squarely on the beat. It should also be emphasized that the grace notes have no time value, are soft in volume, and that their time is "stolen" from the beat immediately preceding the drag.

Procedure for teaching and learning the *drag* should follow that outlined in the section on the flam.

For loud drags use full arm strokes. When less volume is desired use lower stick arcs on the main notes. Very soft drags are made by using wrist taps on the main notes.

Note: Stickwork remains the same when drags are called for as for single strokes, i.e., grace notes are not counted when determining sticking arrangement.

Common Faults—Drags

1. Drag not felt as a unit.
2. Grace notes too loud in relation to main note.
3. Grace notes assume a rhythmic significance.

THE RUFF

Ruffs are grace note combinations played with single alternate sticking. Ruffs serve as a means of thickening or broadening accented notes.

The 4 Stroke Ruff

In practice the 4 stroke ruff is most commonly used. A well known instance is Meacham's *American Patrol*, which contains an opening snare drum solo passage consisting entirely of 4 stroke ruffs. This solo, incidentally, is difficult to play because of the *pp* volume indicated.

The key to playing good 4 stroke ruffs is to make the three grace notes as quick and unimportant sounding as possible, "stealing" time from whatever note or rest precedes them, and aiming for the main note which must fall precisely on the beat. Ruffs are difficult to execute in rapid succession, but fortunately are not very often encountered in a series. A typical usage is the final chord of a march:

In learning the 4 stroke ruff, practice first the R ruff and then the L, slowly at first. Practice alternated ruffs only after good stick control has been achieved. The object of practice should be the exact control of the timing of the three grace notes so that the main note will fall squarely on the beat.

Practical playing techniques of professional percussionists often vary considerably from the pure rudimental tradition. The 4 stroke ruff is a case in point. Two commonly used substitute stickings are:

The foregoing substitute ruff stickings are used when 1) time does not permit the alternate sticking of the authentic ruff, and 2) when a more closed sound is desired than could be obtained using single sticking.

In practicing the first of these substitute ruffs

♫♩ ♫♩
RRL R   LLR L

be sure to make the grace notes sound clearly as a true triplet. Avoid this rhythm ♫♩ ♫♩ .
RR L R   LL R L

The second of the substitute ruffs should sound like an extended drag. It may be practiced open, in which case fine stick control will be necessary to produce an even triplet with all notes sounding. As applied in performance, this extended drag is usually closed. Since the grace notes will then sound like a buzz no exact number of sounds can be distinguished by the ear.

As to the question of interpretation of the written

figure , the performer's skill and good judg-

ment will be the determining factors in deciding whether to use the authentic 4 stroke ruff or one of its two possible substitutes.

THE PARADIDDLE SERIES—SINGLE, DOUBLE, TRIPLE PARADIDDLES

The word "paradiddle" is an onomatopoeic carry-over from the rudimental era when such phonetic devices were used to teach drumming by rote. In the

single paradiddle:

The paradiddle has no characteristic rhythm; it is merely a method of sticking which gives a slightly different sound than would the same group of notes played with normal alternated sticking. Paradiddles are a combination of single and double sticking, with a double pair of notes final in each.

The double paradiddle is a six note group:

The triple paradiddle is an eight note group:

The paradiddles are treated in this *Guide* as a technique for developing good stick control, and not as important rudiments of snare drumming. Indeed, they need never be used for interpreting band or orchestra drum parts. Rudimental solos, however, often specify paradiddle sticking for groups of six-teenth or eighth notes.

Each paradiddle set should be practiced in steady sequence, very slowly at first. It takes more than a

little practice to play the paradiddles, and there is great stick-control value because of the ever-present challenges of speed and evenness. When practicing for speed make certain that the last two doubled notes are not crushed but sound as two distinct notes.

The accenting indicated in the examples shown in the left hand column is only one of many possibilities. For example, the permutation of the single paradiddle would yield:

A good individual or class project is to write out and play the permutations of all three paradiddles. There is hardly a better stick control study. Many professionals use various treatments of the paradiddle series as warm-up and daily practice routines.

An interesting study in progressive meter change follows from the paradiddles when they are played l'istesso tempo. The 2/4, 3/4, 4/4 measure signatures result.

One of the chief musical values of paradiddles (aside from the fact they make fine flexibility studies for the percussionist) is the different sounds they produce for a given grouping of notes through their use of alternate and double sticking. The variations on the paradiddle sticking pattern, although, strictly speaking, themselves not paradiddles, are useful tools to utilize when attempting to blend phrase-wise and match articulation with an ensemble. The following are examples of such variations and are good stick control studies:

FLAMADIDDLES

The addition of flams to each of the accented notes in the foregoing example results in the so-called Flamadiddles.

In the interpretation of rudimental drum solos, the performer is obliged to use the paradiddles when they are designated in the score. For most players performing band and orchestra drum parts, alternate sticking will provide a more rhythmically secure sound; however, players should be mindful of the paradiddles' value in attempting to blend with an ensemble. Perhaps the paradiddles' chief inherent value to the modern day percussionist is as stick control builders.

THE RATAMACUE SERIES—SINGLE, DOUBLE, TRIPLE RATAMACUES

Similar to the paradiddle series, the ratamacues are a legacy from the rudimental tradition. The origin of the word is also onomatopoeic as applied to the single ratamacue:

The ratamacues are compounded of drags and triplets, with a final single stroke. The accenting is usually on each drag, but may also be withheld until the final single stroke. Thus:

The single ratamacue is most logically written in 2/4 signature.

The double ratamacue has one additional drag, of the same hand, at the beginning:

The double ratamacue may also be accented on the final single stroke. It fits naturally into a 3/4 measure.

The extension of the ratamacue series provides the triple ratamacue:

It may be accented on the final single stroke also.

The possibility for playing a l'istesso tempo series of single, double, and triple ratamacues is similar to that illustrated in the section on paradiddles. Two-quarter, 3/4, 4/4 meters follow each other quite naturally to correspond to the number of beats in each ratamacue.

Practice each ratamacue slowly, with open drags, at first. There is no particular purpose to be served by running the ratamacue series for high speed. It is better thought of as an exercise for development of *clean* drags and *good* triplets. Bring out the accents wherever they are placed.

THE FLAMACUE

The flamacue is an additional example of the value of the ancient rudiments as technique builders. The flamacue as such is rarely met with in orchestra or band scores, however it is often incorporated into rudimental drum solos. Its practice is recommended for the purpose of developing a fine degree of stick control. The flamacue is written:

In practicing the flamacues the trick is to displace the natural accent from the initial flam to a good solid accent on the single stroke which follows it. This will require slow practice at first. The flamacues should be practiced hand-to-hand. Note that the stickwork pattern is strict alternation.

Clean flams are called for in the flamacue, and watch particularly the final 𝅘𝅥𝅮𝅘𝅥 in the group. Make it closed, and on time.

THE SINGLE STROKE ROLL

The single stroke roll is listed in the NARD* chart as among the 26 American drum rudiments, yet it is likely that the perfection of the very rapid and exciting single stroke roll is of fairly recent development among the drumming fraternity. Logically, the single stroke roll is but an extension of the alternate single strokes and taps which, it has already been pointed out, constitute the very fundamental technique of snare drumming.

Sustained single stroke rolls are rare in concert music, but short groups of 𝅘𝅥𝅯𝅘𝅥𝅯𝅘𝅥𝅯𝅘𝅥𝅯's are sometimes executed as single strokes by skilled drummers. An example from the orchestral literature is Rimsky-Korsakov's *Sheherazade*, fourth movement: (See illustration A at bottom of page.)

In dance music, jazz, and particularly Latin-American music the single stroke roll is used extensively for fills, endings, and timbale beats. A single stroke roll so rapid that it approaches the sound of an open double stroke roll is a basic part of the jazz drummer's repertoire.

The notation of the single stroke roll appears in the NARD rudiment chart as: (See illustration B at bottom of page.)

In practicing this rudiment it is well to start with slow full arm strokes, accelerating gradually and at the same time reducing the stick arcs on down through the wrist taps to the point where only the hand and finger movements activate the sticks. Practice should aim at attainment of maximum speed, therefore, proceed as far as possible, i.e., until the evenness and control break down. Follow this effort with a few seconds of rest in order to relax the arm, hand, and finger muscles, then start the procedure over again.

There is, of course, a physiological limit to the speed attainable and this limit will vary somewhat from one individual to another. Few students, however, approach their actual limit. Only with assiduous practice can the single stroke roll be brought to a high degree of *controlled* speed. A useful psychological approach to practice is to think of *pushing ever beyond* the present rate, even though it may seem that from one day to the next no increase in speed has been achieved. Results of diligent practice can usually be noted more realistically on a week-to-week or month-to-month basis.

SPECIAL SNARE DRUM TECHNIQUES AND EFFECTS

Rim Shots. There are two generally used methods of producing rim shots on the snare drum. The first method employs both sticks. The rim shot is made by holding the L stick so that the tip rests at or near the center of the drumhead and also makes contact with the rim midway down its shaft. This L stick is then struck sharply on the top of its shaft just below the L hand grip. See Figure 3.53.

In addition to the crossed-stick method, there is a second way of making the explosive sound of the

repeat 4 times

R L R L R L R L R L R L etc.

*National Association of Rudimental Drummers.

rim shot. It is simply to strike the drumhead and rim *simultaneously* with a single blow of the stick. Either stick can be used. See Figures 3.54 and 3.55. A fine control is needed to catch the rim and head simultaneously, as the slightest misjudgment in the angle and either the head or the rim will be struck and no rim shot will result. Dance band drummers usually favor this second method of making rim shots because it does not require the use of both sticks at the same time. For any rim shots which might be called for in a band or orchestra part, however,

Figure 3.54. Rim shot, single R.

Figure 3.53. Rim shot, crossed-stick method.

Figure 3.55. Rim shot, single L.

the first method is usually best because it is safer and there is nearly always plenty of time for its execution.

Rims, play on rims, or S.D. rim. The direction *rim* when marked on a snare drum part is not to be confused with rim shot. What is intended is the striking of the rim of the snare drum only. The sticks are held in regular snare drumming position, except that their angle is changed in order that the shoulders of the sticks strike the drum on its rim. The sound produced is rather brittle, "ticky," and nonresonant.

On the shell. "On the shell" is like "on the rim," a direction to be taken quite literally. Execute any passages so marked on the shell of the drum with regular snare sticks.

Au bord. Au bord is a direction which, translated from the French means "at the edge" or "near the edge." For any passage marked *au bord*, play about one to two inches from the edge of the drumhead. This will produce a soft, veiled tone. It is often used by the composer when he wishes the drum to convey the idea of sound coming from a long distance.

Senza cordes. Senza cordes means literally "without snares." To get the proper sound in passages so marked throw off the snares. On field drums with no lever mechanism for quick snare throw-off, a handkerchief or other small cloth can be inserted between snares and snare head to prevent the snares from vibrating.

Muffled drum. Muffled drum is the English equivalent of *senza cordes*, i.e., drum with snares disengaged.

Muffled drum does *not* mean damp the drum tone with a cloth on the batter head. Muffled street drums are traditional in any marching done in a cemetery or at any service of a memorial nature.

Damping. There is some ambiguity of meaning in the term *damping* when applied to the snare drum. As the term is consistently used in this *Guide,* damping of the snare drum would indicate that the tone is to be stopped instantaneously by sudden pressure of the finger tips on the batter head. In actual practice such a direction is never included in drum parts, staccato marks or "sec" being common ways of implying that the drum should be damped. If a direction is found to *damp drum* or "dampen drum," the player should place a handkerchief on the upper portion of the batter head. This will serve to cut down the resonance of the drum. If it seems desirable to cut the drum's natural resonance still further, place a wallet on the drumhead.

Wire Brushes, or **Brushes.** The snare drummer in the band or orchestra will have occasion to use the wire brushes, either when called for in the score or when providing a modern sounding rhythm background for arrangements of pop tunes. The brushes are held in the same way that snare drumsticks are held. To get the full-sounding "swish" used by dance and jazz drummers, one brush is rotated on the drumhead while the rhythm figure is played with the opposite brush. One much-used beat is:

where the L brush is rotated clockwise twice per measure around the outer circumference of the head. The R brush keeps the basic jazz beat going, starting with the first count down at the lower portion of the head and moving across the rotating L brush for the ♪ , back to its original position for the ♪ and staying there for the ♩ which starts the cycle over again.

For a more extensive discussion of brush techniques, see Chapter 9, *Dance Band Drumming.*

Figure 3.56. Using brushes on the snare drum.

STYLE IN SNARE DRUMMING

A point of snare drumming not often fully realized by the inexperienced player is the matter of style. Generally speaking, the "open" style of playing is proper for martial music such as marches, fanfares, and flourishes. By open style is meant that the flams, drags, rolls, and other rudiments should be executed in a fairly open manner. In particular, the roll should not be too "fine," too crushed or pressed sounding. The stick rebounds should be more perceptible and the individual taps and bounces more audible. The field drum responds well to such openness of playing. Indeed, the appropriate open style for military music stems from the origin of the snare drum rudiments as military flourishes and cadences.

Conversely, music found in the concert band and orchestra repertoire which is not martial in character demands a more closed (refined, delicate) treatment by the snare drum player.

It might be well to mention here that the correct choices of drum, wire or gut snares and drumsticks are also very important factors in obtaining an appropriate tone and style in the various musical contexts. The marching band will, of course, employ field drums exclusively. The style of playing for field work is properly the open, rudimental style with plenty of full arm stroking. A heavy stick should be used for parade work, as WFL 2B or S1. Gut snares are usually considered best for marching band.

The concert band usually employs both field and concert type snare drums. In marches and heavy passages the field drums will be useful, *but* they should not be used in the playing of more delicate snare drum passages such as are found in many concert overtures, dances, and transcriptions of orchestral works. The 6″ or 8″ deep concert snare drums should be used for these passages, with snares of gut or wire, or the new combination wire-gut snares. The 2A, 4A or 5A sticks will be best for concert snare drums. Avoid the too-light 7A models. Many symphony orchestra drummers prefer a rather heavy stick on the concert drum, such as the Leedy #20.

In the orchestra the most crisp, responsive and sensitive snare drum available should be used. The preferred drum currently is the heavy metal-shelled 5½″ or 6″ model, equipped with gut snares. Rarely should more than one snare drum be used in unison. The style of playing should be closed, with the roll as "fine" as possible. The major problem in orchestral snare drumming is attaining the control demanded to play *softly* enough without losing control. The most difficult kinds of passages are the soft, rapid series of single strokes or taps, and the *pp* roll, especially when these occur as solos. These two problem techniques should be practiced on the drum rather than on the practice pad. The goal of practice is: soft volume *and* precise rhythm.

Some composers have scored for *military drum* in symphonic orchestra compositions. Passages so marked should not be played on the small orchestra drum but on a gut-snared field drum mounted on a stand.

Dance band style is treated separately in Chapter 9, *Dance Band Drumming*.

SNARE DRUM NOTATION

Clef. When the snare drum part is printed on a staff the 3rd space of the F clef is used. If for some reason another line or space is used, the part is marked *S.D.* In many contemporary works the various percussion instruments (non-pitch) are printed on single lines in order to save space. Some composers and percussionists are advocating the use of the neutral clef sign for the percussion instruments of indefinite pitch. Perhaps the use of the neutral clef is "splitting hairs," however, it does offer a way of cancelling the treble or bass clef signs when a percussion part changes from a pitched to an unpitched instrument. An example of each of the four usages is given following:

Roll Notation. There are several ways in which a roll can be indicated, by far the most common being the three slanted dashes through the note stem:

Note: the eighth note flag counts as one dash.

Occasionally in older music the trill sign is used to denote the long roll:

A third roll indication is four slanted dashes through the note stem. It is rarely seen nowadays. It is interpreted exactly as any other roll sign:

A fourth and newer method (however not widely used) of indicating not only a roll, but also that the composer desires the roll to be of the very closed, multibounce type is a symbol in the form of a "z" occurring over the note head or on the stem of the note:

Note well, however, that *not all* slanted dashes signify a roll. A single slanted dash indicates that the note is to be played as 8th notes:

A pair of dashes signifies that the note is to be divided into 16th notes:

The two foregoing abbreviations are easily misconstrued as rolls. A further note: the usual three-dash roll sign does not necessarily imply 32nd notes, although this would seem to be the logical inference. It simply means that the drum tone should be sustained by means of the roll technique for the duration of the note, and in the style dictated by the music.

An accent mark over a roll means to accent the attack:

The use of ties in connection with roll notation has great significance for the drummer. In the typical case a long roll will both begin and end *on the beat*—often ending on the next, or a later, strong beat. A tie connects the note (single tap) which is the end of the roll:

This concluding tap is accented naturally, or can be written with the accent sign >. It will nearly always be a R tap. It must fall cleanly on the beat. Much experience is necessary before the student will automatically adjust his wrist alternations to enable him to come out on the concluding single tap "right on the button."

If the long roll is written so that it does not end *on* the beat but extends up *to* the beat, no accent is made on the final single tap. The roll should ideally stop *just ahead of* the next beat. For students, a convenient and clean way of ending such rolls is to conclude on the final "and" count. This is a nice point of interpretation. Common practice among professionals is to roll as close as possible to the next beat when playing in a slow tempo where a gap would be noticeable, and to end on the final beat, or half-beat, if the tempo is fast. The measure

can be played in at least three ways dependent on the tempo:

Occasionally rolls are seemingly incorrectly written, that is, a tied-over sound would be better than a break in the rolls, and vice versa. For example:

As notated it is correct to break between each of the

here, but if the ensemble has legato chords

this would be better played:

Phrase with the ensemble in cases where rolls are ambiguously notated. Remember, the final arbiter is the ear.

Occasionally, "literal" or "measured" rolls are called for, i.e., the exact number of strokes as indicated by the note subdivided into 32nd notes. This is usually indicated by preceding the roll notation with one unit completely written out such as follows:

Grace Notes. Grace notes encountered in snare drum music are summarized in the following table:

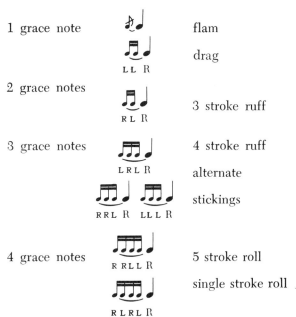

1 grace note		flam
		drag
2 grace notes		3 stroke ruff
3 grace notes		4 stroke ruff
		alternate
		stickings
4 grace notes		5 stroke roll
		single stroke roll

5 grace notes   single stroke roll
L R L R L R

6 grace notes   7 stroke roll
L L R R L L R

single stroke roll
R L R L R L R

8 grace notes   9 stroke roll
R R L L R R L L R

Stroke Roll Designations. In rudimental drum literature, figures are often placed above short rolled notes to indicate which of the stroke rolls to use. Do not take these figures too literally! The correct choice of short roll *depends upon the tempo.* Obviously, at a slow rehearsal tempo the 7 or 9 stroke will be necessary to fill the time-slot occupied by a 5 stroke roll at a bright march tempo. Of course some adjustment in degree of openness can compensate for minor tempo variations. The point is that in the actual performance situation the choice of roll is a matter of individual judgment. The important thing is to fill the time-slot with sound.

Adding Flams. In some cases composers and arrangers leave the addition of flams to the discretion of the player, especially in marches where flams are most appropriate. In general, the part should be played *as written* until the wishes of the conductor can be determined.

Abbreviations Commonly Found in Snare Drum Music

5—	5 stroke roll
7—	7 " "
9—	9 " "
11—11	" "
13—13	" "
15—15	" "
17—17	" "

Br.—brushes
R—right
L—left
R.S.—rim shot
s.c.—senza cordes (without snares)
S.D., Sn. Dr., —snare drum
X—stick beat

For foreign language terms for the various types of snare drums see table, Chapter 2, pages 11 to 23.

CHAPTER 4

Bass Drum
and Cymbals

GENERAL DESCRIPTION

The bass drum sound is a unique component of the total band, orchestra, marching band, and dance band sonority. With its lowest frequencies it puts a foundation on the ensemble. Both rhythmic and timbre functions characterize the bass drum. In metrical music like marches and dance-like pieces it can truly be considered the "heartbeat of the orchestra." Bass drumming is demanding in its musical, technical, and physical requisites. A bass drummer who takes his work seriously and plays with fine musicianship is that rare gem which most instrumental directors seek but seldom find. One reason for this situation is that, after having learned snare drum technique, the bass drum appears to the average student to be a bore. A selling job is often required in order to develop student interest in the bass drum. An instrumental director therefore must take care to show a full measure of regard for the importance of this instrument. He may easily find examples in almost any type of musical literature which demonstrate the importance of the bass drum. For example, in marches the band could function without the snare drums, but might flounder rhythmically without the solidifying pulse of the bass drum. The policy of rotating snare drum, bass drum, cymbals, and timpani assignments within the class or the percussion section of the orchestra and band will give all a chance to gain experience in bass drumming, and will enable the director to pick the student showing particular aptitude for the important concert assignments.

There are several important points to be made in connection with the instrument itself before considering its playing techniques. First, the bass drum should be of a size appropriate to the ensemble. The following table summarizes the recommended dimensions for various types of instrumental ensembles:

Elementary school band or orchestra—14″ x 28″.

Complete concert band and symphony orchestra—16″ x 32″—38″.

Marching band and drum corps—10″ x 28″.

Dance band—14″ x 22″, or 14″ x 20″.

Courtesy Ludwig Drum Co.

Figure 4.1. Bass drum, 14″ x 28″, single tension.

The bass drum should be of the double tension variety (each head can be tensioned separately). It should have two good live heads, either calfskin or

62

Figure 4.2. Concert bass drum on rack, 16" x 34", double tension.

Figure 4.4. Scotch style bass drum, 10" x 28".

Figure 4.3. Concert bass drum mounted on an adjustable tilting bass drum stand.

Figure 4.5. Dance band bass drum, 14" x 22", showing muffler and foot pedal.

plastic. To aid in making the choice between calfskin and plastic, some helpful information is given in the Chapter 3 section on drumheads. Generally speaking, the same considerations apply to snare drum and bass drumheads on the question of calfskin vs. plastic.

A cradle or rack is necessary to bring the bass drum up to its playing position. All major drum manufacturers market a folding metal rack, but these are not entirely satisfactory because of the tendency of

the heavy vibrations of the drum to rattle the braces of the rack. This type of rack, if used, should be padded with felt or other soft material in order to prevent distracting vibrations. A cradle made of wood cut to the exact specifications of the particular drum is a better mounting for the concert bass drum. Also available on the market is an adjustable tilting bass drum stand. (See Figure 4.3) This stand is highly recommended. It permits the performer to select the exact proper playing position for the drum to achieve maximum control and tonal effect. It facilitates executing rapid two stick parts and rolls. It also aids in positioning the bass drum for multipercussion playing. Web slings are necessary to carry the marching band bass drums, and are included in the purchase price quoted in the catalogs of the leading makers. The dance band bass drum requires a foot pedal equipped with a hard felt, cork, or wood beater.

TUNING BASS DRUMHEADS

The unsatisfactory sound of so many school bass drums is caused by *too much tension* on the heads. For concert playing, the bass drum should have a low, indiscernible pitch. Heads tuned too tightly will not produce the low partials that are necessary to give the drum its characteristic, resonant sound. On the other hand, if the tension is too loose, the drum will have a lifeless, slapping sound.

There are two approaches to tuning a concert bass drum. One is to tune both heads to the same low "pitch," the other being to tune the heads to separate "pitches." The latter method has the advantages of producing a sound of resonant quality with many overtones and quite indefinite in pitch. As an example of this method of tuning, let us consider the steps taken to tune a 34″ bass drum. With the left head completely muffled, tune the right head to a low E. Then muffle the right head and tune the left head to a low E♭. Obviously, the pitches will vary with different size drums i.e., lower pitches being used for larger drums and conversely, higher pitches being used for smaller drums; however, the minor second interval between the two heads should be maintained.

To insure that bass drums utilizing calfskin heads in areas or periods of low humidity will be flexible enough to obtain the desired sound, tighten each tuning rod two or three half turns *after* each playing period. Then at the beginning of the next playing period loosen each tuning rod (an equal number of half turns) until a good low, resonant tone is obtained. The reverse of this process should be used in areas or periods of high humidity. This procedure will insure enough slack flexibility in the heads so that a good tone can be produced in any kind of weather. Care should be taken to see that each tuning rod is turned an *equal number of half turns*. As with all drumheads, tension must be kept equal at all points around the perimeter of the head. If this rule is followed unfailingly from the time a new head is put on, the rims will remain equal at all points.

Marching band and drum corps bass drumheads, in contrast to those on concert band and orchestra instruments, should be fairly tight and since both heads are played upon, they should be tuned to the same pitch.

Dance band bass drums are usually tuned to produce a rather dead sound. The heads should not be tight, the exact amount of tension being a matter of personal preference. In addition to the tension, dance band bass drums require muffling devices. Nearly all bass drums made specifically for dance work come with a round disk-type muffler covered with soft felt which attaches by means of a clamp to the rim. It should be mounted so that it contacts the playing head. If the drum still has too much after-ring, and most do, it has been found that one or two strips of flannel stretched across the inside of one or both of the heads eliminates most of the undesired ring. The step-by-step procedure for installing the flannel strips is:

1. With bass drumhead down on floor, remove the counterhoop (rim) and playing head.

2. Cut a strip of cloth about two or three inches wide, about six inches longer than the diameter of the drum.

3. Stretch the strip across the shell slightly to the right or left of the center line.

4. Fit the head over the shell so that it holds the cloth strip snug against its under side.

5. Remount the counterhoop and put a small amount of tension on each of the tuning rods.

6. Cut off the excess cloth which protrudes on each end.

7. Apply final tension.

Experimentation will show the number and placement of cloth strips necessary to get the characteristic dead tone associated with dance band bass drums.

A third device used by drummers to achieve a satisfactory tone is a patch of moleskin stuck onto the playing head at the spot where the foot pedal's beater strikes the drum. Moleskin is a soft felt-like fabric backed with an adhesive plaster, and is obtainable in any drug store in small packages of 4 to 6 sheets. One sheet, which is approximately 3″ x 5″, is right for the purpose. Drummers today prefer to use a hard beater whose impact sound is softened by the moleskin patch rather than the fluffy lamb's-wool beaters which were once popular.

BASS DRUM NOTATION

The bass drum notes are most commonly written in the first or second space of the F clef, with their stems pointing down. In much of the standard band literature the snare drum, bass drum and cymbals are all scored on the same staff, as in the following examples:

In these examples the snare drum plays the upper notes and the bass drum and cymbals play the lower notes *in unison*. This is customary procedure for marches, dances, overtures, etc. In some of the newer band literature and in most orchestral scores the bass drum is written on a separate staff, often on a separate part. In such cases the staff or part is clearly marked *Bass drum, B.D., Bass Dr.,* or one of the foreign equivalents. (See table Chapter 2.) Occasionally the bass drum notes are written on a single line in the interest of saving space. It is customary for their stems to be pointed down, but there are many exceptions.

Rolls on the bass drum are indicated by the use of three slanted dashes through the note stem 𝄽 .

The trill sign is sometimes used, especially in older music 𝆖 .

In cases where the bass drum and cymbals play from the same notes, the composer or arranger indicates by the abbreviations *B.D.* and *cyms., cybs., cbs.,* or *cym.* when he wishes the bass drum or cymbals to play alone. After such note or notes, the abbreviation *Tog.* is used to indicate that the two instruments are to resume playing together. An example of such usage is:

As a general rule bass drum notes are written with some regard for their actual duration. That is, if the composer wishes long booming tones he will use long value notes, as

If he desires a shorter, crisper or "deader" sound he will usually, if he is careful in such matters, write short value notes followed by rests, as

The player strikes and damps the drum in accordance with the style of writing. Staccato markings under bass drum notes mean to damp the tone very quickly.

THE PLAYING SPOT

No hard and fast rule can be adopted which will stipulate the correct playing spot on the bass drum. Variable factors are the size and shape of the drum itself, condition and characteristics of the heads, the atmospheric conditions of the moment, kind of beater used, style of the music, volume of tone desired, and so on. Most often one will find that the bass drum sounds best when struck at a point midway between the center and the rim. Most players find it convenient to locate the playing spot in the upper portion of the head when the drum is in playing position. Some very fine players are known to prefer the lower portion of the drum, however, allowing the arm to hang more or less straight down.

The drum is rarely struck at dead center, this being a nonresonant point on any circular vibrating surface. For certain effects, however, even this center spot is utilized. Trial-and-error experience is the only real help in determining the optimum playing spot on a particular drum in a particular passage of music.

HANDHOLDS AND BASIC STROKES

The handhold for the bass drum beater is made by grasping the beater about ⅓ of the way up from the butt end of the handle (where it feels balanced) with the right hand, thumb on top, fingers curled loosely around the stick. See Figure 4.8.

Figure 4.6. Upper playing spot.

Figure 4.7. Lower playing spot.

Figure 4.8. Bass drum handhold.

At least three major, and many minor, variations in the manner of making the stroke on the concert bass drum are in common use. The first can be described as a straight stroke style. To play in this manner one strikes the drum direct blows, varying the arc of the beater ball and the playing spot on the drumhead to obtain gradations of tone and volume. The wrist and arm are brought into play, with the wrist action providing the resiliancy needed to produce a good tone. For the very loudest sounds, upper arm and shoulder muscles activate the stroke.

The second style of bass drum stroke is the glancing blow. Players who use this style employ the handhold as just described. Using a sharp wrist snap, the head is struck on the return, or "up" phase of the ellipse described by the path of the beater ball. The playing spot is in the upper portion of the drumhead at a point near the player's chest. If a very hard tone is required the arm and shoulder muscles are brought into play. In playing regularly recurring beats, as in a march, the arcs described by the beater ball should be kept equal to insure evenness of timing and volume. In rapid tempos equal *up and down* strokes are used by many players, each motion including a wrist snap which causes the beater ball to brush the head with a glancing blow.

A third style of bass drum stroke is made by allowing the arm to hang down at a natural angle while striking the drum with fairly direct blows, tending toward a "pulling up" motion on each stroke. The playing spot for this method of bass drumming lies in the lower portion of the head. See Figure 4.7.

The question arises as to which of the three styles should be adopted and taught. Among professional players in symphony orchestras the second method is rarely seen. The finest symphony players prefer either the first or third style, both of which are essentially *direct* blows. Percussionists with high school and college band training almost invariably use the glancing blow style, often incorporating fancy wrist flourishes into their strokes. Such motions are not only considered good showmanship, but their pendulum-like function is probably an aid in stabilizing the timing of the beats.

In the author's opinion the direct blow style is best, and should be taught both to band and orchestra percussion students. For one thing, it is basically a more natural action. Secondly, the notion that a bass drum should be struck a glancing blow to produce its proper sound is contrary to the accepted manner of striking nearly all of the other instruments of percussion. Thirdly, a glancing blow simply does not impart maximum vibration to a drumhead. It must be pointed out, however, that the resiliency of the blow (or stroke) to any percussion instrument is of the utmost importance. Once a stroke has been administered to an instrument, any lingering of the beater on the surface of the instrument impedes the free vibrating of that surface and drastically inhibits tone production. Hence, the use of the "glancing" approach is understandable when trying to teach the "resiliency concept" to a student.

The correct playing position for the bass drummer is shown in Figure 4.9.

Figure 4.9. Bass drum playing position.

Notice that the left hand is kept out over the head opposite to the batter head. In this position it is ready to contact the head in applying the light muffling action utilized when playing soft passages, and it is ready to apply the sudden inward pressure used to

damp the drum after a short note or on a cut-off from the conductor. The slight left hand finger contact just mentioned helps to control the amount of ring to the tone of the drum, and should be used most of the time when playing at *pp,p,* or *mp* volumes. See Figure 4.10.

Figure 4.10. L hand muffling bass drumhead.

A completely different conception of bass drumming is evident in the so-called Scotch style of playing. College marching bands whose major duty is to provide football spectaculars usually feature one or more bass drums played in the Scotch manner. It is a flashy technique using two beaters made of hard felt equipped with leather thongs which loop around the player's wrist and fingers and thus may be twirled between strokes. For added flash, crossover beats are possible in which the R beater strikes the left head and vice versa.

The dance band bass drum is played by means of a foot pedal. When the toe is depressed a spring arrangement pulls the beater ball forward, making contact with the drumhead. The pedal beater comes in handy in studio band work and is often utilized in the pit for musical shows, ballets, and light operas where one percussionist must play timpani, bells, xylophone, chimes, etc., and also double drums. In such situations there is always the problem of having too few hands, so that bass drum notes played by the foot make it possible to use both hands at the same time on the timpani, snare drum, cymbal, or even a mallet instrument. The term "double drums" was coined during the vaudeville pit orchestra era to refer to the then new set-up which permitted one man to play both snare and bass drums through the invention of the pedal. The term is still used.

THE BASS DRUM ROLL

The preferred method of executing a roll on the bass drum is with a pair of timpani sticks. The standard snare drum handholds are used, and the L is held from a position above the drum pointing down parallel with the playing surface. The R is held in the normal way. The roll is produced by making rapidly alternating *single* strokes, and in this respect is like the timpani roll. With the use of a

Figure 4.11. Bass drum roll, timpani sticks.

tilting stand and the drum in a horizontal position, the matched timpani grip and style of playing may be conveniently utilized. A matched pair of small bass drum beaters, rather than a pair of timpani sticks, is preferred by some bass drummers. The goal of practice should be control of the timing and the volume so that a smooth roll at any volume level is obtained.

Avoid using the double-ended beater to produce a roll. It produces an uneven sounding roll.

DAMPING

The bass drum will continue to ring distractingly if it is not completely damped on both heads the instant the tone is to be stopped. To damp the bass drum the player must place the palm of the left hand and the wrist and finger tips of the right hand (the beater must still be held) quickly onto the centers of the heads and press inwards. Another method of damping which allows great control is to damp the right (playing) side of the bass drum with one's right knee, while damping the left side with the left hand in the manner mentioned above. For this method, the player rests his right foot on the drum rack or other convenient object. The drum should be damped at all cut-offs from the conductor, during rests, general pauses, and after notes marked *sec.*, or *secco*, staccato notes, and at the conclusion of long tones which are being allowed to sound for specific durations. The bass drum should *not* be damped after a note followed by a slur mark, as this is the usual method of indicating "let ring." Control of duration is not as precise when playing the bass drum by means of the foot pedal. About the only way to damp the tone in this case is to press the pedal very firmly on, or immediately after, the short note. The contact of the beater ball on the head will serve to damp the tone to some extent.

MISCELLANEOUS POINTS—BASS DRUM

1. A variety of bass drum beaters should be available to the player, including double-ended lamb's wool for general use, a pair of soft felt timpani sticks or a pair of matched beaters for rolls, a hard felt beater for obtaining a good staccato, a pair of Scotch bass drum sticks for field work, and a wooden-ended stick, such as WFL 344 timpani sticks, which are felt at one end and wood at the other.

2. The range of volume obtainable on the bass drum is very great. Accenting thus may run the gamut from subtle, lightly accented tones to cannon booms and thunder peals. Any written-in accents should be carefully observed by the bass drummer in order to extract the maximum musical effect from the otherwise monotonously regular patterns. Anyone who has ever heard a topnotch military band bass drummer will appreciate the skill in accenting by means of which the player literally creates his own part, furnishing a rhythmic drive to the band not obtainable by any other means.

3. Do not be afraid that single notes marked *solo* will be too loud if played with full power. Exploit the "bombs"—they are exciting.

CYMBALS

General Description

The clashing tone of the cymbals has been one of the most exciting timbre ingredients in music for many centuries. Oriental and near-eastern music featured cymbals long before the dawn of recorded history. It is a well known fact that the best producers of cymbals have been the Turkish artisans. Early in the Classic period of music, Haydn and Mozart introduced these "Turkish Music" instruments into the symphony orchestra. The foremost makers of cymbals are the Zildjian family, whose father-to-son traditions include a secret formula for mixing the alloy from which the cymbals are made. The Zildjian family's products have dominated the world market since 1623. The family business split in 1929, one brother moving to the United States and the other remaining in Constantinople. It is supposed that the formula used by each is identical. The Avedis Zildjian Co. is the U. S. manufacturer. All Zildjian cymbals bear the imprint identifying them as K. Zildjian (the Turkish manufacturer) or Avedis Zildjian. In the paragraphs to follow much of the material has been drawn from an article "Sounding Brass and Cymbals" which originally appeared in *The Music Journal* and can be obtained from the A. Zildjian Co., N. Quincy, Massachusetts, in pamphlet form. The author is Robert Zildjian.

Every cymbal of high quality contains virtually every tone, with attendant upper partials. The variation in tone among individual cymbals is due to the relative strengths of certain of the fundamental and partial tones in each. No single tone should dominate the sound of a cymbal. The only variance between different cymbals of a similar type lies in their *dominant* pitch and in their different reactions to sympathetic vibrations. The response of some cymbals is faster than others of the same category. This means that one cymbal reaches full vibration sooner than another. There is no such thing as a cymbal tuned to a C, or D, etc. (The tuned antique cymbals, or crotales, are an exception.) The only difference, pitchwise, is that some cymbals produce a generally high aggregate sound, others being medium or lower in relation.

Cymbals to be used as a pair clashed together should be selected to *blend* with each other, not to *match* in general pitch. The complimentary sounds produced by two carefully matched cymbals is spoken of as a "marriage." Thin cymbals are usually lower in pitch than medium or medium heavy. There are exceptions, however, which may account for the common misconception that the opposite holds true. The quickness with which the cymbal reaches full vibration ("speaks") is dependent upon the amount of metal in the cymbal, therefore thin and small cymbals are usually the fastest.

The most popular sizes of cymbals for elementary and junior high school bands and orchestras are 14", 15", 16", and 13" in that order. This may serve as a rule of thumb when purchasing cymbals for such groups. The most common mistake made by persons responsible for the purchase of school instruments is to buy cymbals which are too small and too heavy. The present author therefore recommends 16" diameter cymbals which are *thin* or *medium thin* (the weights are stamped on the back of all Zildjian cymbals) for general use in elementary band and orchestra. Heavy cymbals are more martial and solemn in tone without the brilliant upper overtones, and are preferred for use in drum and bugle corps.

For the high school, college and professional concert band and orchestra a pair of *medium* or *medium thin* 18" concert or symphonic cymbals are standard equipment, paired to obtain a compatible blend of tone. The trend today is toward *medium thin* to obtain the lightness and brilliance of the so-called "French" tone. In addition to a pair of 18" cymbals, the high school or college band and orchestra should have one pair of matching band cymbals 16" to 18", one pair of large, medium thin cymbals 20" to 22", plus two or three smaller cymbal for suspended cymbal use. These should probably include a 14" thin, 17" thin, and 18" medium cymbal. This basic list will cover the requirements of the repertoire of most musical organizations.

There are two other types of cymbals which have certain specialized uses. The first of these are called antique cymbals, or crotales. They are small, thick cymbals which come in pairs ranging from 2" to 5" in diameter. They have definite pitches through a chromatic two octave range. The sounds produced are of great clarity and have an ethereal beauty. The edges are struck together to obtain their characteristic tone. Certain Impressionistic Period works, notably Debussy's *Afternoon of a Faun*, specify antique cymbals, as do several of the experimental compositions of contemporary composers. The second type of small cymbals are the so-called finger cymbals. These are small untuned cymbals about 2 inches in diameter, much thinner than the antique cymbals. The manner of playing is the same as for the antique cymbals. Finger cymbals can be mounted on springy wire handles which can be squeezed together to contact the faces of the pair of cymbals. They are then called metal castanets by the manufacturer. Figure 4.12 shows each of these types and several pairs of antique cymbals.

The assortment of cymbals for the dance band drum set which has been developed by Zildjian are designated as Bounce, Bounce-ride, Ride, Crash, Be-Bop, Fast, Splash, Sizzle and Swish. A Bounce, Bounce-ride, or Ride is used for open stick work in playing

the basic jazz beat ♩ ♫. ♩ ♫ . These types

come in weights running from medium heavy down to extra thin. A Crash cymbal is used for single note crashes and is not made for prolonged riding. The preferred weight for the crash cymbal is thin. The

so-call Be-Bop cymbals are specially tapered to build up a heavy sustained tone when played with the single stick ride rhythm. Drummers usually prefer a large diameter, 19″, 20″, or even 24″ for this purpose. The Sizzle cymbal has rivets placed around the outer edge which vibrate when the cymbal is struck, and are useful in jazz work as a change of sound from the ride cymbal in sustained rhythm. Swish cymbals are similar, but their edges are turned up, which imparts a "pangy" Chinese sound. Dixieland jazz drummers are the chief users of the Swish type of cymbal. The paired Hi-Hat (also called sock, or hi-sock) cymbals are mounted on a stand and operated with the left foot. They ching together on the afterbeats in dance and jazz music. They should be of medium thin or thin weight, and the preferred sizes are 14″ and 15″.

Cymbals are somewhat delicate, especially the thin, paper-thin, and extra-thin weights. They are easily cracked and bent at the edges, so they should be handled with care. Cymbals should never be thrown into a "trap box" or bin, and they should

Courtesy A. Zildjian Co.

Figure 4.12. Metal castanets, upper left. Finger cymbals, lower left. Antique cymbals at right.

never be left lying on the floor where a false step might ruin them. If cymbals are to be transported often they should be carried in the mackintosh zipper bags made for the purpose. Cymbals should never be buffed on a wheel, as the heat generated by the friction can remove the temper from certain areas of the cymbal's surface, causing them to go dead. To clean cymbals, use a low- or non-abrasive cleaner such as Bon Ami or Copper Clean.

To remove small cracks at or near the edge of a cymbal, drill a small hole about ¼" in diameter slightly beyond the end of the crack. Hacksaw a V shaped piece out which includes the portion containing the crack. Saw right up to the drilled hole, and smooth off the sawed edges.

Wooden handles should not be used for the pair of cymbals. They are usually too rigid and they kill a good deal of the brilliance in the cymbals. Leather or rawhide straps are the best holders for the band and orchestra cymbals. Avoid the fluffy lamb's wool pads which are used to protect the knuckles of the player. Less of the tone is stifled by using felt pads, which can be cut out of any fairly heavy felt. The steps in tying the cymbal strap knot are as follows:

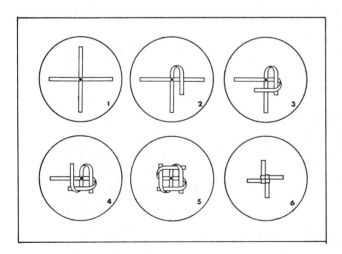

Figure 4.13. Tying cymbal strap.

Note: The knot itself should be tight, but not the bind of the strap through the cymbal. The straps should feel somewhat loose in order to allow maximum vibration.

CYMBAL NOTATION

When cymbals are played as a pair, one clashed against the other, the Italian word *piatti* (literally, *plates*) is used to describe both the cymbals and the

style of playing them. Piatti is a useful term because it differentiates the pair of cymbals clashed together from a single cymbal struck with a stick or other beater.

In much standard band literature, and some orchestral music of the lighter variety, the cymbals play in unison with the bass drum. Sometimes the part will be so marked, but often the percussionist must assume that such was the composer's intention. As can be seen in the following illustrations, the cymbals play from the notes written in the first or second space of the F clef. The note stems point down.

In this type of scoring for cymbals and bass drum, when either is to be played alone, the part will be marked "Cyms. only," (cyms) or "Bass drum only" (B.D. only, B.D., etc.). This may apply to a single note,

a phrase, strain of a march, movement or entire composition. After a note, phrase, or strain indicated for either B.D. or cymbals *alone*, the abbreviation *Tog.* (together) is used if the composer wishes both the B.D. and cymbals to play the succeeding notes together. A diamond-shaped or X-shaped notehead is often used for solo cymbal notes, as:

Modern notation is getting away from this by assigning a definite line or space to the cymbal part and using normal noteheads. Unless otherwise specified, cymbal parts are played piatti style. *Suspended cymbal, susp. cym., one cym.*, etc., are directions indicating the use of a single cymbal mounted on a floor stand and struck with a drumstick, mallet or timpani stick. Also, any roll or trill sign on the cymbal part indicates the use of the single cymbal played with sticks or mallets.

Roll signs for cymbal notes are conventionally the three slanted dashes through the note stem, or the trill sign.

It is possible to approximate a sustained roll-like sound using the pair of cymbals, but it is not a very satisfactory effect. When the composer deliberately specifies this style of roll he uses such directions as "rub cymbals together," "clashed cymbal roll." This type of roll is made by rotating the pair of cymbals in opposite directions while allowing their edges to be in light contact.

A tie or slur mark after a cymbal note means to let the cymbal or cymbals ring beyond their indicated value. If an unlimited after-ring is desired, the direction "let ring" or L.V.—let vibrate is given in the part.

Let ring
(L.V.)

A variety of sticks and beaters can be used to obtain interesting sounds on the suspended cymbal. If there is no indication in the part to the contrary, the suspended cymbal is struck with a timpani stick or a vibraphone mallet. The indication "wood stick" or "with SD stick" means to strike the cymbal with a drumstick. Commonly found foreign language directions are: "avec baguette de bois" (with wood stick), "avec baguette d'eponge" (literally, with sponge-headed stick, however, notes so marked should be played with soft felt timpani sticks).

Other beaters which are called for on the suspended cymbal are the wire brush, xylophone mallet, triangle beater, and even a fingernail file (Milhaud's *Aubade*)! When such exotic beaters are indicated the score will be clearly marked to show the notes which are to be struck with the particular beater.

Abbreviations Commonly Found in Cymbal Music

piatti—the pair of clashed cymbals
cym, cymb, cyb, cymbs, cb, cbs—cymbal, or cymbals
susp. cym.—suspended cymbal
secco, or sec.—dry, short
chk.—choke (damp)
X—cymbal note (older form of notation)
L.V.—let vibrate

BASIC STROKES

To play the pair of clashed cymbals requires considerable physical strength as well as good musical sense. The cymbal straps are grasped in the manner illustrated in Figures 4.14 to 4.18. Note that the hands *do not go through* the loops of the straps. Young players will invariably put their hands through and wrap the loops tightly around their wrists. Such a manner of holding is actually quite clumsy and is too tight to allow the cymbals to vibrate fully. However, for reasons of security in maintaining the grasp and for the purpose of twirling the cymbals, the hands may go through the loops for marching.

To play steady beat passages, as in a march, the cymbals are held out in front of the player's chest. They are struck one against the other with their outer edges *almost*, but not exactly, coinciding to produce the sound on the beat. If there is an exact coincidence of the two cymbals, a suction will result which embarassingly holds the pair of cymbals together and produces nothing but a dull "plop." To avoid this locking, make sure that the cymbals ease into contact, leading edge first.

Experienced percussionists do not usually move both arms alternately up and down, as would perhaps seem natural. Instead, their cymbal stroke is made by holding the left cymbal in fairly stationary position, slanted with the top edge toward the left, and bringing the right cymbal alternately into up and down contacts against it. In passages where the notes are widely spaced, or for single notes, the same position is used, but all the strokes are "down," or, more exactly, "down and out." Figures 4.14, 4.15, and 4.16 show the ready position for such a cymbal stroke and the position of the cymbals just after impact.

Gradations in volume are obtained both by changing the velocity of the moving cymbals and by the amount of edge placed in contact. For the very softest cymbal tones, it is possible to barely "ching" the top edges of the pair together. If the player will take the pains to practice, he can learn to control the cymbal contacts to the point where pianissimo notes can be played using the entire circumference of the cymbals. This is really a much better sound than the aforementioned top edge contact, but it takes fine neuromuscular control and an intimate knowledge of the particular properties of the pair of cymbals being used. To increase the volume, the right cymbal is moved faster and travels a longer path. For loud single crashes, the right clashes with considerable speed at impact. The left cymbal, rather than remaining stationary as it does for soft notes, draws in and away at impact, so as to separate the cymbals.

Figure 4.14. Ready position.

Figure 4.15. Start of stroke.

Figure 4.16. Finish of stroke.

For widely spaced notes or solo single crashes the player must give careful thought to the volume and duration appropriate to the passage. For a long and prominent after-ring the cymbals should be brought up and faced toward the conductor by turning the wrists. The extending of the arms up to a position about head high and slightly in front of the player will accomplish the best results. This is sometimes called the *flare stroke,* and is useful for projecting the tone in solo crashes. To start the flare stroke, drop both cymbals to a position slightly in front of either thigh, bringing the cymbals into contact with a rapid upward sweep, and follow through by turning the wrists so that the cymbals face the conductor. The trajectory of each cymbal is similar for the left and right in the flare stroke. Figures 4.17, 4.18 and 4.19 show the ready, impact, and final positions of the flare stroke.

Another type of stroke can be called, for want of a better name, the *separation* stroke. This type of stroke is made by placing the edges of the pair of cymbals into contact silently prior to the time the note is to be played. To sound the cymbals, move them in opposite directions. The contact of their edges will produce an ethereal "ching" as the cymbals are separated. The effect is rarely called for, although it is truly beautiful in sound. The volume in the separation stroke is controlled by the speed of the motion used.

TECHNIQUES OF PLAYING THE SUSPENDED CYMBAL

One cymbal used alone is an indispensable part of the percussion equipment in band or orchestra. Many scores call for suspended cymbal, although nowadays

Figure 4.17. Ready position, flare stroke.

Figure 4.18. Impact.

Figure 4.19. Finish of flare stroke.

the old style hook-like arm arrangement has been replaced by the dance drummer's cymbal floor stand. What is required, in any case, is a good quality crash cymbal mounted on a floor stand about waist high.

Figure 4.20. Suspended cymbal struck with snare drumstick.

For single note crashes on the suspended cymbal using a snare drumstick, strike the edge of the cymbal sharply at about a 45° angle. For a less harsh impact, percussionists in symphony orchestras often strike the suspended cymbal on its top surface with a yarn-covered vibraphone or marimba mallet. Figure 4.21 shows the suspended cymbal played with a xylophone mallet. Always have the left hand free to choke the cymbal after a crash. Do not choke, or damp, the cymbal if the note has a slur mark after it or is marked "let ring." Damping is accomplished simply by grasping the edge of the cymbal firmly. With both drumstick and mallet beaters much variation in tone and volume can be obtained. Experience is the

best guide in obtaining the musically appropriate sound in a given passage.

Another style of suspended cymbal playing is sometimes called for, namely, the striking with the tip of the drumstick on top of the cymbal. This is similar to the bounce or ride cymbal technique of the jazz player, except that the rhythm figures will vary. The sound is completely different from that of the crash. It is useful in very light passages. See Figure 4.22. A number of sounds can be obtained, depending upon which part of the surface is struck. A "ting" sound can be produced by striking the suspended cymbal on the dome section, using either the tip or shoulder of the drumstick or a triangle beater.

Figure 4.22. Suspended cymbal struck with tip of drumstick.

One additional little used but interesting manner of playing the suspended cymbal is to drag a metal object such as a triangle beater or key across the cymbal's surface from the dome out to the edge. See Figure 4.23.

Figure 4.21. Suspended cymbal struck with xylophone mallet.

Figure 4.23. Suspended cymbal played with triangle beater.

THE CYMBAL ROLL

The roll is often called for in cymbal parts. For this reason the suspended cymbal must be considered standard equipment. The single stroke roll is used. The cymbal is struck rapidly alternating blows on its top surface with yarn marimba sticks or mallets. In order not to knock over the cymbal stand when playing a loud roll, place the two mallets at opposite sides of the cymbal. Occasionally cymbal rolls are marked to be played "with S.D. sticks" or simply "wood sticks." In this case snare drumsticks held in the usual manner are used to make a double stroke roll on the surface of the cymbal. This will cause the higher frequencies in the cymbal tone to predominate, producing a more "tinkly" sound than does the mallet technique.

A variety of drumsticks, timpani sticks, and vibraphone—marimba—xylophone mallets should be at the disposal of the cymbal player.

A hint regarding the mounting of the suspended cymbal: do not let the wing nut be screwed down tight, as it is imperative that the cymbal be riding as freely as possible. Any slight bind or pressure is likely to damp out the high frequencies which give cymbals their brilliance.

DAMPING

To damp the cymbals when played piatti style, the player has merely to draw in the vibrating cymbals to make contact with his clothing at the front of his shoulders. This stops the sound instantaneously. See Figure 4.26.

Figure 4.24. Suspended cymbal roll with mallets.

Figure 4.26. Damping the pair of cymbals.

Figure 4.25. Suspended cymbal roll with snare drumsticks.

It behooves the cymbal player to use care in observing the notation of his part. If a short value is used, or staccato marks are present, very quick damping is called for. If the note is of a long value, allow the cymbals to ring at least for the duration of the note before damping.

The suspended cymbal is damped by grasping it firmly with the left hand.

The cymbal part may sometimes show a slur or tie

extending over a rest, such as—

This means to let the cymbal or pair of cymbals ring somewhat beyond the value of the note. If the composer or arranger desires the cymbals to ring indefinitely, the direction "let ring" or L.V.—let vibrate is printed over or under the note.

CHAPTER 5

The Mallet-played
Instruments

GENERAL DESCRIPTION OF THE XYLOPHONE, MARIMBA, VIBRAPHONE, BELLS, BELL-LYRA (GLOCKENSPIEL) AND CHIMES

The Xylophone. The prototype xylophone was a crude set of tuned wooden bars laid flat upon a bed of straw developed around 1500 in Europe and called the strohfiedel (German for "strawfiddle"). Its primitive ancestors probably date back many centuries to African and Javanese origins. One J. Gusikow was the first virtuoso of the strohfiedel, and in 1830 aroused the interest of Mendelssohn. It was not until nearly fifty years later, however, that the xylophone was actually introduced into the symphony orchestra by Saint-Saens in his famous *Danse Macabre*.

As an improvement over the bed of straw, the bars were later mounted on a wood frame and this frame laid on a table. The next development was a floor stand to accomodate the frame and bars. Tubular metal resonators are often added to the modern instrument, but they are not always present, and indeed, are not necessary for production of a true xylophone tone. The characteristic sound of the xylophone is hard, brittle, and incisive. Its tone quality derives from the thick rosewood bars and the hardness of the mallets used to strike these bars. The xylophone has a thin tone and lacks carrying power when soft rubber or yarn-wound mallets are employed. The bars are laid out in the keyboard arrangement corresponding to the keys of the piano, with the lower bank of bars containing the natural tones and the upper bank the chromatics. For convenience of execution the upper bars extend slightly over the lower ones.

A good size of xylophone for school use is a three octave c' to c''' model, with or without a floor stand and resonators. Many xylophones are made with a 3½ octave range, f to c''', and of course these added notes are a convenience in eliminating the

Courtesy G. C. Jenkins Co.

Figure 5.1. Xylophone.

need for frequent octava sopra transpositions in the low register. A fibre carrying case is a good investment if the instrument is subject to a good deal of portage.

Figure 5.2 shows the bars of the standard 3½ octave xylophone and their corresponding written pitches. The xylophone sounds one octave higher than written.

The xylophone requires hard mallets. At least two pairs would be needed for all-around use, one of medium hard rubber and the other of very hard rubber or plastic. Good xylophone mallets are hard to find, and should be selected personally at a drum shop rather than ordered from a catalog, as it is nearly impossible to know in advance what a mallet will sound like from the pictures and meager descriptions furnished in the manufacturers' catalogs. The handles of most xylophone mallets are made of rattan or plastic.

Figure 5.2. Xylophone keyboard.

Courtesy G. C. Jenkins Co.

Figure 5.3. Marimba.

The Marimba. The marimba is essentially a xylophone equipped with resonators to increase the volume and resonance of the bars. There is some evidence that the marimba dates back to primitive cultures both in Africa and Central America, where gourds mounted beneath the bars were found to amplify and mellow the natural sound of the hardwood. While the xylophone may or may not have resonators, the marimba always has them. There is one other essential difference in that the marimba bars are cut somewhat thinner than xylophone bars to make them more elastic, thus imparting a more resonant sound. The keyboard layout is the same for both the marimba and xylophone, although as a rule the marimba will have one or more octaves more than the typical xylophone. The additional notes of the marimba are dictated by

Figure 5.4. Marimba keyboard.

the solo demands of the instrument and the four-mallet style often used in solo playing. The marimba is particularly effective in its lower register. Two, three or four note chords struck singly or tremolo sound rich, mellow and organ-like. In its upper register the marimba sounds about like a xylophone, perhaps a little mellower. The marimba is not often scored for in band and orchestra music, as it does not have a quality which penetrates as does the xylophone. The marimba therefore has become essentially a solo instrument. Marimba ensembles are fairly popular also. A good marimba for school purposes should include the fourth octave (c′ down to c), making the total range c to c′′′. The marimba should be mounted on a stand with casters for mobility in solo use. Figure 5.4 shows the bars of the 4 octave marimba and their corresponding written (actual) pitches. In the 1960's the marimba gained stature as a result of

the serious concert efforts of Vida Chenoweth and other marimba virtuosi. Paul Creston has written a delightful and challenging *Concertino for Marimba and Orchestra,* and Robert Kurka composed a marimba concerto before his untimely death. Aside from these listed examples and a few more isolated works, original literature for the instrument is sadly lacking. Its repertoire consists largely of transcriptions or arrangements of works written for other monodic treble clef instruments.

The marimba should never be played with the very hard, uncovered rubber mallets used on the xylophone. Not only will the rich mellow sound of the marimba be lost thereby, but the very hard rubber mallets can dent and throw out of tune a marimba bar. One or two pairs of medium or soft uncovered rubber mallets and two pairs of yarn covered marimba mallets are essential basic items.

Figure 5.5. Vibraphone.

The Vibraphone (Vibraharp). The vibraphone, sometimes called vibraharp, is the most recent development in the mallet-played instrument group. Its two most prominent distinguishing characteristics are its electrically driven fans mounted at the top of each resonator to impart alternating loud and soft pulsations of the tones, and its damper pedal mechanism. With its rotating fan-like blades it gives the illusion of a vibrato in its tone quality, but the "vibrato" is of intensity only, not pitch. The bars are made of aluminum alloy, whose metallic tone further distinguishes the vibraphone from the wood-barred instruments. As can be seen in Figure 5.5, the upper bank of bars does not extend out over the lower, as in the xylophone or marimba. The reason that this is so is in order that the upper ends of the natural bars can lie in such a way as to contact the felt damper bar, while the lower ends of the chromatic bars contact the same damper felt. The "vibra" mechanism is not always used, many of the modern jazz players preferring the cool sound of the straight tone. In concert band and orchestra scores directions such as "motor on," "motor off," "vibré" and "non vibré" indicate to the player when to use each effect. A small switch mounted near the upper end of the instrument turns the motor on and off. When the motor is off, strict attention should be paid to the fans in order to determine whether or not they are in a "closed" or "open" position in relation to the bars and resonators. They should be in an "open" position and can be manually turned to that position if they already are not so aligned. Most models also have a device for controlling the rate of speed of the fans. Amplification, at an added cost, also is available for newer models.

The most popular size of vibraphone is three octaves, f to f′′′. This is the recommended instrument for all purposes. Figure 5.6 indicates the written (actual) pitches of the standard three octave vibraphone bars.

Figure 5.6. Vibraphone keyboard.

The usual mallets used on the vibraphone are the yarn-covered type. The core of these mallets is of rubber, the handles of rattan or plastic. The relative hardness of the rubber core is what determines the tonal quality of the mallet. Most models come in hard, medium and soft strengths. Plain rubber mallets give a clicky, pingy tone and are therefore seldom used except for practice. There are, however, many varieties of vibraphone mallets on the market. One of these consists of a sponge rubber disc mounted at the end of a heavy wire handle. Another variety has its hard rubber core covered with a closely knit yarn "stocking." Still another type is string-wound. The best policy is to try out a set of mallets on a vibraphone before purchasing them. The player should have at least two sets at his disposal.

The moving parts of the vibraphone should be kept lubricated with a light oil such as 3-in-1. Also, the instrument should be kept covered when not in use to prevent accumulation of dust around the moving parts. It is a good plan to keep an extra rubber drive belt on hand, as these items frequently break or get misplaced. The bars can be kept shined with ordinary silver or metal polish.

Courtesy G. C. Jenkins Co.

Figure 5.7. Bells.

Bells. The small bells used in the orchestra and band are variously called *orchestra bells, glockenspiel,* and *campanelli.* The set of bells consists of steel bars mounted in the keyboard fashion, usually attached to wooden frames mounted directly within the carrying case. The sound of the bells is clear and yet "tinkly," and they are quite penetrating when played with metal bell hammers. The bells are the most often used mallet-played instruments in school music scores. Most of these bell parts are fairly simple technically, and a pianist may sometimes be impressed into service to cover the part. All members of the band and orchestra percussion section should become acquainted with the bells and learn to locate the bars according to the notation.

With regard to size, the bells are probably the most consistent of the mallet percussion instruments. With the exceptions of the Parsifal Bells developed specifically for the Wagnerian orchestra and some older three octave models, they now are almost exclusively of one size: 2½ octaves from g to c''' (written pitch). They sound two octaves higher than written. Figure 5.9 indicates the written pitches of the bars on a three octave set of bells.

For the orchestra bells, the small wheel-shaped metal hammers with rattan handles are best but are hard to find. Pyralin, hard plastic, or hard rubber mallets are most common, and can be ordered from manufacturers' catalogs. The rubber or plastic types of bell mallets are good for softer passages, but quite a bit of click is usually audible on impact.

Bell-lyra. The bell-lyra, often called glockenspiel, is a marching band version of the orchestra bells. The typical model consists of 25 steel bell bars mounted in a tubular lyre-shaped steel frame with the keyboard running from low to high as the instrument is extended in front of the player. The bell-lyra is carried in a holster which is attached to the player by means of a harness similar to those used by flag bearers. The instrument is usually played with one mallet, doubling the melody in marching music. A very rigid holster has been developed recently which supports the entire weight of the bell-lyra at the proper playing angle so that both hands can be used. The major difficulty in playing this instrument lies in accustoming oneself to the outward-running keyboard.

Courtesy G. C. Jenkins Co.

Figure 5.8. Bell-lyra.

Figure 5.9. Bells keyboard.

The keyboard of the bell-lyra is shown in Figure 5.10. Note that the two octaves span a to a′′, sounding two octaves higher than written.

The bell-lyra is played with hard plastic mallets.

Chimes. The chimes, sometimes called tubular chimes, are indispensable items in the concert band or symphony orchestra. The tone quality of the chimes resembles that of the carillon bells associated with church music. Their tone is sombre yet stirring, and is therefore often used by composers to suggest religious and patriotic moods. An example of the former usage is Puccini's one act opera *Suor Angelica*. Ravel employed the chimes effectively in his orchestration of the *Great Gate of Kiev* from Mussorgsky's *Pictures at an Exhibition*.

Today, chimes are commercially, available in two sizes from c′ to f′′, and from C′ to G′′. They sound as written.

Chimes have a unique overtone series that differs from the overtone structure of all other musical instruments. This, primarily, accounts for the great amount of controversy to be found concerning the transposition of this instrument. In order to simulate the out-of-tune sound of bells, the chime tone contains many frequencies, particularly at the moment it is struck. These various frequencies or overtones rapidly decay leaving three main pitches. For example, if c′ is struck, we hear both a predominant c′ and c′′ along with a rather strong out-of-tune sixth below. Due to this peculiarity, we experience much confusion concerning the transposition of this

Figure 5.10. Bell-lyra keyboard.

instrument. The chimes should be considered a non-transposing instrument.

The standard chime mallet is of laminated leather or wood and looks like a small mall. For most chime parts, one mallet will suffice, but some passages demand two. A chime rack is indispensable. The type with padded holes through which the tubes pass is best, since this device prevents the tubes from swaying under impact of the mallet and clanging with adjacent tubes. The best modern instruments have a damper pedal similar in action to that of the vibraphone. This gives a big advantage to the player, as it frees one hand from the duty of damping nonchordal tones individually. Two-mallet technique is thus greatly facilitated. Figure 5.11 shows a one and one-half octave set of chimes with damper pedal. This is the recommended instrument for school, college, and professional use.

COMMON CHARACTERISTICS AND DISTINCTIVE FEATURES OF THE MALLET-PLAYED INSTRUMENTS

With the exception of the tubular chimes, the mallet-played instruments are essentially vibrating wood or metal plates. The acoustical properties of vibrating plates need to be known to the player of these instruments. The most resonant point of the bar is its center. Nodal points are nonresonant areas which are located at approximately the points where the bars attach to the frame. Half way between the nodal points and the ends of each bar are located resonant spots which are useful playing spots. See Figure 5.12. In playing chromatic passages on the mallet instruments, the natural notes should be struck at the center of the bar for maximum resonance while the playing spot on the chromatic bars will be located half way between the near end of the bar and the point at which it attaches to the frame. By utilizing these nearer playing spots, much unnecessary motion is eliminated.

The basic handhold is the same for all the mallet instruments when played with two mallets. Each is grasped in the same way as the R snare drumstick, at a point slightly more than ⅓ of the way down from the end of the handle. Ready position for the mallets is about 1 to 1½ inches above the bars. The L mallet should strike above the R if both are on the same bar. If both mallets are playing successive notes on one of the chromatic bars, the left will play skips up or down. Figures 5.13 to 5.15 show various playing positions for the pair of mallets.

Figure 5.13. R and L on natural bar.

Figure 5.14. R on chromatic bar, L on natural bar.

Figure 5.15. R and L on chromatic bar.

Figure 5.11. Chimes.

at the center and the right at the playing spot at the near end of the bar. To produce a good tone the mallets must strike the bars with a resilient blow. A rather sharp forward snap of the wrist activates the stroke for both R and L. The arms are involved only in notes of the very greatest volume or in long

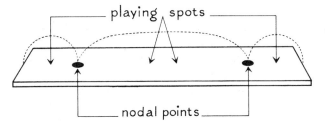

Figure 5.12. Playing spots, xylophone, marimba, vibraphone, or bell bar.

The major technical problem in playing the mallet instruments is the development of a kinesthetic sense of intervallic relationships. The mallets must travel through space and land accurately on the correct bar and proper playing spot. Sample sequential studies for the development of interval accuracy follow. They may be practiced on the xylophone, marimba, vibraphone, or bells.

1. Scalewise melodic movement

5. Slowly

Study #6 illustrates how cross-overs may be avoided by using *successive* rather than *alternate* sticking.

6.

7.

8.

9.

Practice Study #10 without rolls at first, thus:

etc.

10. Slowly (♪ = 104)

Another facet of the interval problem is the difficulty encountered when changing from one instrument to another. An instrument with wide bars, considerably separated, will require longer reaches than an instrument with narrow bars and close spacing. This difficulty is not as great as one might suppose, however, for the reason that the ear plays a large role in the kinesthetic process as it relates to pitch and distance in these instruments. A skillful player needs only a few seconds of warm-up orientation to change rapidly from one instrument to another.

In teaching the techniques of the mallet instruments, the instructor should insist upon a minimum motion of the mallet. Recall that the ready position for each stroke is 1 to 1½ inches above the bar. The mallet head will then travel upward slightly before striking. The mallet should not be held up 6, 8, or 12 inches above the keyboard prior to the stroke. It is a useful concept to think of the mallet arriving at its destination of an inch or so above the bar as long as possible in advance of the sounding of the note. If this concept is developed through slow practice of intervals, it will facilitate accurate technique later in the playing of rapid passages.

A problem inherent to the mallet instruments, and which can become quite critical if not corrected at the outset of instruction, is that of the use of the eyes. Performers on mallet instruments must develop split or peripheral vision so as to encompass the keyboard, the music, and the conductor. Any beginning mallet player will have a strong tendency to look at the keyboard as he plays. If this is not

corrected, it will result in his failing to watch the conductor and greatly impede his reading ability. Peripheral vision, rather than direct eye contact with the keyboard, should be developed. Then, the constant shifting of the eyes from music to keyboard will not be necessary.

The xylophone, marimba and vibraphone are played from a standing position. In order to keep the mallets directly in front of the body where they are most easily controlled it is necessary to shift the body weight from one foot to the other when changing registers of the keyboard. The three and four octave instruments are so long that a step or two to one side or the other is often required to maintain a balanced playing position. The player should not stand erect, but lean slightly toward the keyboard. The bells can be played from a sitting position if it is more convenient to place them on a low table or stand. For the usual small set of bells no appreciable shifting of body weight is necessary. The chimes are played from an erect standing position.

The distinctive tone qualities which characterize the various mallet instruments have already been mentioned. Because of these distinctive tonal features each of the instruments has become identified with certain typical idioms. Composers and arrangers do well to develop a firsthand knowledge of the best idiomatic usage for each of the mallet-played instruments.

The xylophone is at its best in dry, brittle, percussive melodic lines. It should not be overworked in any one composition, as its tone is monotonous if too long continued. Two-note chords, called "double stops," are commonly found. The tone can be sustained by means of a roll, which is a rapidly alternated series of single strokes. High velocity passages of chromatic or diatonic scales and arpeggiated figures are quite playable on the xylophone. Because the vibrations of the bars are of very short duration, the xylophone tones do not blur or build up any appreciable clang.

The marimba is very similar to the xylophone in its technical demands. When played two-mallet style the same velocity is possible. Rolls are executed in the same manner also. The major difference is one of idiom. The marimba bars are more resonant than those of the xylophone, but their tone is less penetrating. Consequently, the instrument is not as useful in the orchestra or band. Because of the longer vibration time of the marimba bars, however, it is ideally suited to legato melodic lines and hence well suited to solo playing. Double stops and three and four mallet chords sound good on the marimba, particularly in its lower register. The technique for holding three or four mallets will be described in the section on playing techniques. To sustain chords beyond their normal single stroke duration a tremolo is used, in which the mallets which play the chord tones are alternated in rapid sequence. Solo literature, both transcriptions of solos originally written for other instruments and pieces composed specifically for the marimba, make extensive use of the tremolo.

The vibraphone has the ability to sustain its tones without the use of a roll or tremolo by means of its free-ringing metal bars and pedal control. The motor-driven vibrato mechanism gives the tone a warm quality that is very beautiful when played alone and also blends well with other instruments. The vibraphone has a greater dynamic range than the other mallet-played instruments. These advantages have made the vibraphone a favorite instrument in the popular music fields, especially in small combo jazz. When the vibraphone first made its appearance in the large studio-type radio orchestras of the 1920's and 1930's, it was pretty much confined to arpeggios and four-mallet chordal passages, coloristic effects, etc. Since that time the trend has been toward a more melodic style. In concert music the vibraphone is used in a variety of ways. Single bell-tone octaves, short melodic lines, and chordal passages are all common. Arrangers of "pops concert" symphonic scores seem to be particularly fond of the lush tones of the vibraphone.

The orchestra bells are at their best on single tones, octaves, and arpeggios. They do not sound good in rapid passages or scale-wise progressions because of the clashes produced by the after-rings of the bars. Slow moving melodic lines are possible, but the player must damp certain tones carefully if he is to avoid unpleasant clashes. Rolls are not often used, as the bell bars continue to vibrate for the value of all but the longest of notes.

MALLET TECHNIQUE

In teaching the mallet instruments one should start with the basic single stroke, which is common to all of the instruments in the group with the exception of the chimes. For a description of the basic single stroke refer back to the paragraphs on Common Characteristics and Distinctive Features of the Mallet-Played Instruments. Note the position of the hands and wrists in Figures 5.13 to 5.15. The single stroke on the chimes is made by tapping the top end of the tube, contacting the "cap" section with the mallet at an angle as shown in Figure 5.16. For most chime notes, a light wrist action is sufficient to produce a good tone. The forearm is brought into play when it is necessary to produce a very loud chime tone.

Figure 5.16. Chime stroke.

The single stroke roll used on these instruments requires much practice in order to achieve the speed necessary for a smooth tone. Slow and even alternate R and L strokes on a single bar prepare the wrist for the later stages of roll development. For control play a series of quarter notes, progressing thence to eighths, sixteenths, and thirty-seconds. The arcs of the mallet heads become shorter as the rate of speed is increased. Gradations of volume are governed by the length of the arcs and the force of the wrist snaps.

Legato playing of rolled note intervals is facilitated if the R mallet is moved to the new bar first when the skip is upward, and the L mallet moved first when skipping downward.

In the tremolo the roll technique is simply split between two notes. Unless the player has developed a rapid single stroke roll on a single bar, this division of the reiterated sounds between two bars is likely to sound rather spotty. On the marimba, particularly in its lower register, the tremolo need not be as rapid as on the xylophone for the reason that the vibration times of the bars are greater, and thus the mallet contacts do not have to renew the vibrations as often to produce a continuous tone.

The handholds for playing with three and four mallets are illustrated in Figures 5.17 to 5.20. Notice that the handles of the *highest* and *lowest* mallets go *over* the other two handles as they are

Figure 5.18. One mallet R, two **mallets** L.

Figure 5.19. Four-mallet handholds, under-view.

Figure 5.17. Two mallets R, one mallet L.

Figure 5.20. Small interval R, large interval L.

held by the thumb and fingers of each hand. The handles remain in contact at this crossover or pivot point. The central problem in four-mallet technique is the adjustment of the width of the angle formed between each pair of mallets so that the desired bars will be struck. This angle adjustment is made principally by the thumb, index, and little fingers of each hand.

To increase the angle of the mallets, slide the thumb forward along the shaft of the inner mallet, at the same time applying pressure with the side of the index finger to the other mallet and pulling the little and ring fingers forward. The position of the outer mallet will remain relatively unchanged. The most difficult playing angle is the very narrow one needed to reach minor and major seconds.

To sustain long tones in the four-mallet style it is necessary to tremolo the notes on the marimba, but not on the vibraphone. The marimba tremolo is made by holding the mallets in a rather loose grip and rocking the wrists in a left-to-right motion while at the same time maintaining the up-and-down alternations. The mallets will then contact the bars in the order L outer, L inner, R inner, R outer. The rate of speed of the tremolo must be great enough to produce the illusion of a sustained tone on each of the bars. This individual contact method of making the tremolo is preferred over the sometimes heard "two and two" style, in which each pair of mallets contacts the bars as a unit. It is a smoother and more musical effect when skillfully performed. It requires much practice to bring under perfect control.

Stickwork. Stickwork, sometimes referred to as hammering, is essentially the same for all of the mallet-played instruments. Normal usage can be stated as a policy: in an ascending scalewise passage, begin with the L and alternate; in a descending scalewise passage, begin with the R and alternate. In chordal contexts and arpeggios, use the L for the lowest tone and proceed upward with alternate mallets—start with the R in similar descending figures. In other words, use the L on lowest notes and the R on the high extremes in any given passage. In between the extremes, alternate mallets are used more often than not. There are certain contours of melodic line which are more easily executed by using successive sticking, i.e., RR, LL. Examples of passages in which alternate and successive stickings are called for are given on page 89. These examples are intended to illustrate *typical* stickwork problems. By applying the principles illustrated in these and the studies on pages 84 to 86, one can develop a systematic approach to mallet playing which will be adequate for all but the most unusual sticking problems.

Damping. Damping is never necessary on the xylophone, seldom on the marimba, and is taken care of on the vibraphone by the damper pedal. The bells (glockenspiel) require damping by the finger tips in order to avoid unpleasant clashes of tones. To aid in phrasing, finger damping is utilized also on the vibraphone. In simple passages where the notes do not succeed each other rapidly it usually is possible to play the notes with one mallet and damp with the opposite hand. When two mallets are required the damping must be done while the mallets are being held in the hands. A light contact with the extended middle finger on the surface

of the bar to be damped is sufficient to kill the tone. If it is necessary to damp suddenly after a sequence of bell notes which are still ringing, run the finger tips of each hand quickly in toward the center of the keyboard making sure that each sounding bar is contacted en route. Another quicker method to damp a series of tones, suddenly, is to place the arms on the keyboard using the L arm on the natural keys and the R arm on the chromatic keys. Do not damp bell tones too soon. Let them ring free at least for the duration of the written value.

Damping on the chimes is accomplished by grasping the vibrating tube firmly with the hand at a point a foot or so below the top end. Not all chime tones should be damped, as often the intention of the composer is to let the chimes build up a clang in the fashion of steeple bells. In many cases the player and conductor must determine whether or not to damp the chime notes. Sets of chimes equipped with a damper pedal simplify the problems of duration of chime notes. The damper pedal when pushed down causes a felt covered damper to contact the tubes.

Figure 5.21. Damping, bells.

MISCELLANEOUS POINTS—MALLET INSTRUMENTS

Solo passages for the mallet instruments contained in band or orchestra scores should be memorized. Knowing such excerpts from memory will enable the player to keep a close eye on the conductor. An excellent source of excerpts from standard literature is contained in Goldenberg's *Modern School for the Xylophone, Marimba and Vibraphone,* published by

Chappell. This same method book also contains copious technical study material presented in graded sequence. It is one of the best volumes of its kind now on the market, and should be in the hands of every student and player of the mallet instruments.

Out-of-tune xylophone and marimba bars must be sent back to the factory for tuning. If they are too far out of tune to be retuned, replacement bars may be necessary. Do not attempt to remove or add wood or other material to an out-of-tune bar in the hope of putting it back into tune. This is a job for the expert.

Frequently the written part for bells, xylophone or other instrument will exceed the range of the instrument at hand. In this case it is necessary to transpose some of the tones an octave up or down in order to bring them into the range of the instrument. Often it is better to transpose a whole phrase or entire passage than to make awkward skips which distort the melodic line. The player should try to keep the passage in question generally high or low, depending on musical judgment to ascertain what sounds best in the particular context. Bell parts frequently sound better when played an octave lower than written, probably because the composer or arranger was unaware that the bells sound two octaves higher than written.

It is a good idea to keep the bars of the xylophone, marimba, and vibraphone covered with fibre board or heavy cloth cut to fit over the keyboard.

Rolls are indicated by three slanted dashes through the note stem , or by a trill sign placed above the note , . This sign would mean tremolo .

The *Xylorimba* is an obsolescent hybrid instrument which was designed to combine the mellow tone quality of the marimba with the penetrating sound of the xylophone. In the three and one-half octave instrument, no longer manufactured, only the lowest octave and a half sounds like an authentic marimba. The remainder of the bars have a distinctly xylophone quality. Boulez' masterpiece *Le Marteau Sans Maître*, written in 1954, calls for a xylorimba.

When the nature of the passage will permit, hold the music in the left hand while playing the chimes with one mallet. There is no convenient place to put a music rack for the chimes, as the tubes obscure the player's view.

CHAPTER 6

Timpani (kettledrums)

HISTORICAL DEVELOPMENT

The kettledrums as we now know them are the product of many centuries of gradual development. They form one of the two main lines of membrane-covered drum development, these two lines being drums with bowl-shaped sound reflecting shells and those with hollow cylindrical shells. According to Sietz[1] the origin of the kettledrum dates back at least to Old Testament Hebrew times. The size and shape of the Hebrew kettledrum is not known, nor do we know whether it was used singly or paired. The ancient Greeks were known to have employed a form of kettledrum in celebrations and rituals. During the Middle Ages, European contact with the Near East resulted in the introduction into Europe of a small-sized version of the timpani called the *naggareh*, or *naggareth*. These kettledrums later became known in France as *nacaires* and in England as *nakers*. They were used in pairs, either carried at the waist of the player or mounted on either side of a horse's shoulders, and became a symbol of affluence and aristocracy. These relatively small kettledrums were known in Europe as early as the thirteenth century.

The direct forerunners of our modern timpani date from 1457, according to both Seitz[1] and White.[2] In this year certain ambassadors of King Ladislaus of Hungary were sent to France to seek the hand of the daughter of King Charles VII. Included in the entourage were "drumes lyke bigge ketels, caryed one on each syde of ye horse's necke." These large drums were played by the performers with an affected grace of style which was to have a great influence on the manner of kettledrumming throughout

Europe during the 16th and 17th centuries. In Germany about the beginning of the sixteenth century the name "tympana" was given to the large kettledrum. In 1542 King Henry VIII of England procured a pair of these large kettledrums from Vienna for use of his cavalry. White cites 1735 as the publication date of the first instruction book, called "Heroic and Musical Art of the Trumpet and Kettledrum." Emphasis was on the "heroics," or elegance of playing posture and manner of striking the drum.

In seventeenth century Germany there were some significant departures made in the construction of the kettledrums which allowed for their later adoption into the orchestra. For one thing, the heads were mounted on hoops and held down by means of metal counterhoops which had several screws placed around their circumference. Clumsy as this first tuning arrangement must have been, it marked the beginning of a truly musical usage of the kettledrums. Early in the ninteenth century handles were added to the tuning screws and their number reduced to six or eight, making tuning quicker and easier. The size of the pair became standardized at this time to approximately the present dimensions of 25″ for the small kettle and 28″ for the large kettle. Illustrations of the time depict timpanists using wooden or ivory-tipped sticks shaped like malls.

Written compositions calling for kettledrums date from 1655. In these early works the kettledrums usually played with an ensemble of trumpets. A common arrangement was to have the three upper parts played by trumpets and the fourth part interchangeable, or doubled, between the fourth trumpet and the timpani. This usage set the trend for scoring kettledrum parts during the Classic period. White credits Lully with the first serious orchestral score including timpani, the opera *Thesée* produced in Paris in 1692. The culminating phase of the Baroque period saw both Bach

[1]Sietz. J. Fred. *Modern School of Tympani Playing*, Elkhart: Leedy Mfg. Co., 1943.
[2]White. Charles L. *Drums Through the Ages*, Los Angeles: Sterling Press, 1960.

and Handel scoring generously and skillfully for the timpani. These masters followed the established principle of tonic-dominant tuning, and used the drums chiefly in conjunction with the trumpets and horns.

Beethoven was the first composer to assign a more independent role to the timpani, even to the extent of writing solo passages of great dramatic impact. He was also the first composer to depart from the strict fourth or fifth interval tunings. In *Fidelio* Beethoven requires the timpani to be tuned to a diminished fifth, and in the Finale of the Eighth Symphony and the Scherzo of the Ninth they are tuned one octave apart.

Both Wagner and Berlioz in the nineteenth century extended the tonal and technical demands on the kettledrums. Both scored occasionally for two sets of timpani to be played by two players. Berlioz can be credited with the development of a variety of beaters for the timpani, and his parts often call for sponge-headed sticks, which he invented for the purpose of obtaining a soft and mellow tone quality. Berlioz' *Symphonie Fantastique* calls for the timpani to be muffled with pieces of cloth placed on the heads—the first use of *coperti*.

During the first half of the twentieth century, both the ranges and the technical demands upon the timpani have increased considerably. The limits of the range are now *great C* to *small B♭*

The best resonance, however, still remains within the octave F to f. In order to reach the extremes of range both above and below these notes it is necessary to employ outsize kettles. For the highest notes a 23″ kettle, called a "piccolo timpani" is used, and for the extreme low tones a kettle 30″ or 32″ in diameter is used. The rapidity with which tuning changes must be effected makes it necessary for the modern symphony orchestra timpanist to use machine-tuned timpani of the pedal, master-key, chain, or rotary types. A description of the commonly used types of timpani, together with recommended sizes, types, and set-ups for various purposes, follows in succeeding paragraphs.

TYPES OF TIMPANI

The simplest and least expensive type of kettledrum is the so-called hand-tuned or hand-screw model. The essential features of the hand-tuned timpani remain relatively unchanged from the kettledrums of the seventeenth and eighteenth centuries.

Tension on the head is adjusted by means of the six screw handles around the perimeter of the bowl. When the handles are turned to the right the counterhoop is lowered, thus stretching the head taut and raising the pitch. The pitch of the head is lowered by turning the handles in the opposite direction. A tripod base is used to set the drum up high enough for convenient playing position. Some models have lightweight metal standard bases which are permanently attached to the bottom of the bowl.

Figure 6.1. Hand-tuned timpani.

Few hand-tuned models are being manufactured today as a result of the demand for timpani which can be tuned more rapidly. It is because of the time required to make a change of tuning (six handles must be turned on each change) and the fact that the player must stop playing in order to adjust the handles that the hand-tuned kettledrum is now obsolescent. They do make good training instruments, however, and can be used in elementary school bands and orchestras where the timpani parts rarely call for rapid changes of tuning.

The most popular type of machine drums (timpani which tune by means other than hand screws) are pedal tuned. There are several varieties of the pedal mechanism, but their common characteristic is a foot pedal which attaches to a vertical rod within the bowl of the drum and is connected to a "spider" of six or eight cables which run to equidistant points on the counterhoop. When the toe portion of the pedal is depressed it lowers the rod inside the bowl, which in turn pulls down the cables which connect to the counterhoop and raises the pitch by applying tension to the head. When the toe portion is raised and the heel is depressed, the reverse process takes place and the pitch of the head is lowered. Pedal-tuned timpani are the most convenient for most players' general use. Their great advantage over any other type is that they can be tuned while both of the timpanist's hands are engaged in playing. For instance, if a long roll is begun which sounds out of tune to the timpanist, he can continue to roll while correcting the intonation by means of the foot pedal. The pedal device is also the fastest type of mechanism so far invented for tuning. The chief disadvantage of older model pedal-tuned kettledrums is that some of the natural resonance of the bowl is lost with the addition of the internal spider mechanism and with the attachment of the heavy metal base. This has been corrected in the newer models with external tensioning systems.

Courtesy G. C. Jenkins Co.

Figure 6.3. Dresden-type timpani.

Courtesy Ludwig Drum Co.

Figure 6.2. Pedal-tuned timpani.

The Dresden type of pedal timpani was developed in Germany and is now also manufactured in the United States. This type combines the tone quality of the best hand-tuned kettles with the convenience of the pedal mechanism. It does this by having all of its moving parts on the outside of the bowl and its bowl supported from the top edges by heavy braces, which allow it to vibrate maximally. The shape of the bowl, being more deep and elliptical than most other types, gives the Dresden timpani a purity and richness of tone unmatched by any other. Another advantage of the Dresden-type drum is its sawtoothed ratchet pedal mechanism which eliminates the problem of slippage sometimes encountered with the ordinary spring balanced pedal. This very advantage can also become a disadvantage, however, as it is necessary to kick out a heel clutch when making a change in the Dresden pedal setting, and this makes tuning slower by a second or two. The main

drawbacks to the Dresden timpani are their high cost and their great weight. They are not practical for other than permanent location use. They are manufactured in this country in sizes 23″, 25″, 26″, 28″, 29″, 30″, and 32″. The best sizes for use as a pair are 26″ and 29″.

Another type of machine-tuned kettledrums is the so-called rotary timpani. The basic principle of this type is that the bowl rests on a large screw, and when the kettle is rotated clockwise an internal spider mechanism pulls downward and thus applies tension to the head, raising its pitch. When the kettle is rotated counterclockwise the reverse action lowers the pitch. Usually two hands are needed to accomplish the tuning, especially in the upper register where the tension is great. This, plus the fact that the best playing spot on the head will not always be available, make the rotary timpani considerably less popu-

Figure 6.4. Standard rotary timpani.

lar than the pedal models. One manufacturer has recently come out with a rotary timpani made specifically for school use which has tuning indicators around the counterhoop which can be preset to show how far to rotate the kettle for each tone. This simple device works well when plastic heads are used, as they are not subject to variation in pitch caused by changing atmospheric conditions.

Several other types of machine timpani are in use, but are not often seen in this country. One such model, which is now being custom made for symphony timpanists by Saul Goodman of the New York Philharmonic Orchestra, makes use of a bicycle-type chain which runs around the perimeter of the bowl and connects with a sprocket at each of the tuning points. When a master key is turned the entire chain moves, causing equal pressure to be exerted on the head at each tuning point. This type of drum has a good tone quality, as there is no internal mechanism or standard base to stifle the resonance.

Persons charged with the responsibility of purchasing timpani for various musical organizations must make a choice from among the several types of timpani, and there are usually questions as to the type of head, new vs. reconditioned drums, etc. The following table is included to serve as a guide in making such decisions. The table should be considered as *suggestion* rather than outright recommendation, as the factors of cost, availability, portability, and personal preference of the player must be taken into consideration when spending the large amount of money required to purchase a set of timpani.

Courtesy G. C. Jenkins Co.

Figure 6.5. Rotary timpani with tuning indicators.

Type of Organization	Recommended Timpani
Elementary School band or orchestra	Pair of rotary timpani, 26″ and 29″ diameters, with preset tuning indicators, plastic heads.
Junior High School band and orchestra	Pair of rotary timpani, 26″ and 29″ diameters, with preset tuning indicators, plastic heads or pair of pedal-tuned timpani, 25″ and 28″ diameters, tuning gauges with plastic heads.
High School band and orchestra	Pair of pedal-tuned timpani, 25″ and 28″ diameters, tuning gauges if plastic heads used, no gauges if calfskin heads preferred also if possible, two outside timpani (for extreme low and high notes) 30″ and 23″ diameters, or 28″ and 25″ if these are more easily procured.
College or University band and orchestra	Set of four pedal-tuned timpani, standard type, or, if budget permits, Dresden type. 23″, 26″, 29″, 32″ diameters, calfskin or plastic heads.
Professional band	Pair of pedal-tuned timpani 25″ and 28″ diameters, plastic heads for outdoor concerts. One or two outside timpani, plastic heads.
Symphony and opera orchestra	Set of four Dresden-type pedal timpani, 23″, 26″, 29″, 32″ diameters, calfskin heads.
Pit orchestra	Pair of pedal-tuned timpani, 25″ and 28″ diameters, plastic heads.

TIMPANI HEADS

Heads for the kettledrums have traditionally been made from the hides of young calves. Within the past few years a synthetic material has been developed in an attempt to solve the problems caused by the calfskin head's susceptibility to change with changes in the relative humidity of the air. These so-called plastic heads have reached a stage of development where they must be taken seriously by school music people and by professional percussionists. Because it still must be considered the standard for judgment, the calfskin head will be discussed in some detail, followed by a discussion of the plastic head, with a summary of the advantages and disadvantages of each to conclude the section on timpani heads.

Calfskin timpani heads are cut from the hides of calves two to eight months old. Because there is a variation in the preferred thickness for timpani heads, the animals used for the purpose are slaughtered at ages varying between the two limits. The process of manufacture is fairly complicated. Suffice to mention that the objective is to produce heads which are extremely elastic, even in thickness throughout, with corresponding evenness of texture. Timpani heads are clear and translucent because they are not pre-stretched at the factory as are snare drum batter heads and bass drumheads. Unstretched heads have greater resiliency, thus enabling the timpani head to stretch and contract enough to obtain the range of a fifth or more when mounted on the kettledrum. The ideal timpani head would show a uniform degree of elasticity over its entire surface, but unfortunately for the timpanist, there are spots even in a good head which will be thin or soft and thus subject to uneven stretching. These minor variations in the timpani head make it necessary for the timpanist constantly to engage in the process of truing up the intonation of his drums during a rehearsal or performance. As to the question of how thick the timpani head should be, there is no pat answer. Some timpanists prefer thin heads and some thick by comparison. The thicker the head the less movement of the foot pedal is needed to change a given interval, but this can work as a disadvantage in the case of semitone interval changes. Presumably thick heads would be stronger than thin ones, but even thick heads will break under certain types of stress. Breakage is usually the result of leaving the instruments stored in a place where they are subject to a sudden extreme change in atmospheric condition.

Plastic heads have been developed, tested, and improved to the point that their sound is most satisfactory. From the standpoint of controlled evenness of texture and thickness, they surpass calfskin heads. The plastic heads have a harder "feel" to the player and the tone, in general, can be described as hard although it is resonant and the vibration time is at least equal to the average calfskin head. Much of this harshness in tone can be overcome by using slightly larger and softer sticks.

In choosing between calfskin and plastic heads, the use to which the particular timpani are to be put is the factor that should govern the selection. Refer back to the table of recommended specifications in this section for suggestions as to the kinds of use which would indicate each type. In general, plastic heads should be favorably considered for use on any timpani which are to be used out of doors. The extremes of variance in relative humidity from the heat of the noonday sun to the dampness of evening not only endanger the life of the calfskin head, but make tuning all but impossible. As a vivid illustration of the difficulties encountered with rapidly changing atmospheric conditions, the author has been in the uncomfortable position of having his drums rise in pitch as much as a perfect fifth during the course of a one hour telecast due to the banks of high-powered lights overhead. With plastic heads there would have been little perceptible change in the pitch under similar conditions. If one is willing to make a slight adjustment in getting used to the different "feel" of plastic heads, and perhaps an ever-so-slight compromise with tone quality, then in many situations the plastic heads should prove superior to calfskin.

A second factor in favor of the plastic head is that it makes tuning easier for the school timpanist. Once set by the instructor or student, the timpani can be depended upon to remain at the pitch indefinitely. Often it happens that, prior to a performance by a young school band or orchestra, the timpani are carefully tuned and checked by the instructor only to have their very first notes sound miserably out of tune and the inexperienced youngster unable to make necessary adjustments. The use of plastic heads would obviate this all-too common problem which plagues every timpanist, be he student or top professional. The plastic head is recommended over the calfskin type for use by elementary, junior high school, and senior high school students because it does not require constant fussy adjustment to keep it in tune.

Note: No matter which type of timpani head is used, the tension must be kept equal at all points around the circumference of the head if a clear tone is to be obtained. *Tuning handles should always be turned an equal amount at each change.* The manner of putting each segment of the head into tune (tuning the head with itself) will be treated in detail in the section on timpani tuning.

One final note concerns mounting calfskin timpani heads. Heads should always be purchased already mounted on the flesh hoops. To mount the head on the kettle, dampen the head on both sides with clear *cool* water up to, but not under, the flesh hoop. Allow the head to dry somewhat until it is limp, wiping off spots of excess water with a towel. Next, place the head on the kettle in such a position that the light strip which runs down the center of the head (the backbone portion) runs between two opposite tuning handles. As the newly mounted head begins to dry, place the metal counterhoop in position, thread the handles, and begin to apply tension at each point. The drums must be watched carefully throughout the procedure lest the drying take place too rapidly. The tuning handles should be turned gradually an equal number of half-turns until the head is dry and produces a good tone on a note in its middle register. *Do not* play on the timpani for several hours after the head has been mounted. It is best to wait until the next day before using the drum.

With a timpani head that has gone dead, or becomes so false that it cannot be tuned accurately, it will usually pay to try to rejuvenate it by the "wetting down" process just outlined for mounting a new head. One variation of the process when wetting down a used head is to let the head dry thoroughly off the drum after the initial wetting, then repeat the entire process. If a head does not sound good after it has been wet down, it should be replaced. Plastic heads are mounted dry and are not ever "wet down." One thing to watch when mounting plastic heads is to see that the top edge of the bowl is smooth and absolutely free from nubs or scratches, as these can tear the head easily. Tallow or lanolin applied to this top edge of the bowl prior to mounting the head will insure that no portion of the head will bind, and it will also eliminate annoying squeaks as the head stretches over the top of the bowl.

PARTS OF THE TIMPANI

Figure 6.6 shows the detail of the timpani bowl, head, hoop, and collar assembly.

The main parts of the timpani are shown in Figure 6.7. Not all models will include all parts il-

lustrated, but the main features of the model here shown are common to all models.

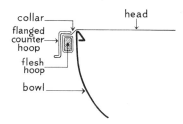

Figure 6.6. Detail of timpani head assembly.

Figure 6.7. Parts of the timpani.

TIMPANI STICKS

The importance of the timpani sticks in tone production is considerably greater than is commonly supposed. By the use of various materials for the beater ball, handle, and inner core, timpani sticks can be made to give a variety of tone qualities. The timpanist needs an assortment of sticks if he is to do musical justice to the parts written for his instruments.

The historical development of the timpani stick is an interesting but little known story. Prior to Hector Berlioz (1803-1869) the kettledrummer was limited to two basic materials for his sticks—wood and ivory. The shape of these sticks was that of a mall, and they must have been somewhat heavier than the sticks used today. It is hard to imagine that all through the Baroque, Rococco, and Classic periods, when so much progress was made in the construction of the instruments themselves and in the musical resources of the parts written for them, the sticks should have remained in such a crude stage of development. Such was the case, and it remained for Berlioz to begin the experimentation which has led to our present day models. Berlioz first tried leather covers over the ends of his sticks but was not satisfied.

As he indicates in his famous treatise on orchestration, "they produce a sound less startling than the preceding (wood sticks), but they are very dry nevertheless." He later experimented with other materials, including mushrooms! Eventually Berlioz settled upon sponge-covered sticks as being the best that could be produced, as he claimed that such sticks could produce a musical, rather than a purely noisy, tone. He described the tone elicited by the sponge sticks as grave and velvety, and indeed they may have seemed so to one accustomed only to the sounds of wood or leather sticks. Berlioz' timpani parts frequently call for "baguettes d'éponge" (sponge sticks), which is correctly interpreted by the modern timpanist as meaning soft felt-covered sticks, not available in Berlioz' time. Felt was eventually found to be the most satisfactory covering material, probably by German timpanists in their never-ending search for the ideal stick.

Most of the better modern timpani sticks are made with straight grained hickory handles and their cork or wood cores are covered with a high quality of damper felt. The handles are about 13½″ or 14″ long and are about ½″ in diameter at the butt end, tapering down slightly to about 5/16″ at the point where the ball is attached.

The choice of sticks is a highly personal matter, and there is a bewildering number of commercially made sticks from which to choose. The main concern of the teacher should be to see that his students avoid the extremes often issued for use in the schools. The very hard solid felt beater ball should be avoided, as it is not a generally useful stick. The other type of stick to avoid is the very fluffy lamb's

Figure 6.9. Wood and double-ended timpani sticks. (l. to r.)

wool variety, which is entirely too "mushy" to produce an acceptable tone. The fact that these latter sticks are relatively inexpensive is not a sufficient reason for issuing them for use by young students. An elastic type handle is not recommended. A rigid handle assists production of the best tone and a clear, concise pulsation. One gets about what one pays for in a commercial timpani stick, and the least one should expect to pay for a pair of sticks at the current prices is $5.00 to $6.00. A good all-purpose stick for school use is one which is of medium hardness, felt disc type. For advanced high school, college and professional players the recommended stick is the Goodman, which, unfortunately, is not available in all music stores. Dealers can write directly to Saul Goodman, c/o The New York Philharmonic Orchestra, to inquire about a supply of these custom-made sticks. They come in five strengths, ball and disc types. The Goodman stick is characterized by its comparatively heavy handle, which tapers uniformly from butt to beater ball, and is made from carefully selected straight grained split hickory.

In speaking of high quality sticks it would be amiss not to mention the Vic Firth line (Vic Firth Enterprises, Symphony Hall, Boston, Mass.) and the Payson line (Payson Percussion Products, 2130 Glenview Ave., Park Ridge, Illinois). The Payson models have a shaft made of an extremely strong, yet lightweight aluminum alloy which will never warp, crack, or split. A special grip surface prevents slipping due to perspiration. The covering on the balls is of 100% surgical felt which is extremely durable. Another fine advantage to these sticks is that the balls are seamless.

Figure 6.8. Super-staccato, medium hard ball type, and disc type timpani sticks. (l. to r.)

In addition to one or two pairs of general purpose sticks, the advanced timpanist should have at his disposal a pair of hard felt-covered sticks (like the Goodman "super-staccato" model shown in Figure 6.8) for playing notes of a very percussive nature, where tone quality is secondary to explosive impact. Another specialized type of stick is sometimes called for, namely the wood stick, the double-purpose stick with one end turned to an olive shaped knob for playing passages marked "wood sticks," "baguettes de bois," "holzschlagel," "col legno." The opening measures of Richard Strauss' *Don Juan* employ the wood sticks for an electrifying effect on the timpani. Stravinsky's *Firebird, Infernal Dance of the Roi Katschei*, features a timpani ostinato played with wood sticks. The model shown in Figure 6.9 is numbered #334 in the WFL catalog.

Timpani sticks need a certain amount of care if they are to give good service. The player should have a special drawstring-type bag made long enough to encase the sticks completely for carrying, or, even better, an attaché case. In addition to carrying the timpani sticks, such cases are useful to carry all manner of sticks, beaters, triangles and other small traps, and also can accommodate music scores and books.

Felt used to cover timpani sticks tends to rough up and form into small nodes. If these fluffy spots are not removed periodically they can affect the tone quality. To trim the excess felt from a beater ball or disc, use a small pair of scissors. Hold the stick in the left hand, rotate slowly while trimming *evenly* around the entire surface of the covering.

In the interest of economy, the timpanist who is willing to persevere with a needle, thread and scissors may wish to recover worn-out sticks. Only a high grade of piano damper felt should be used, the ½" thickness being carefully split into two equal thicknesses. Use the *inner* side of the split felt for the outer covering. Dental floss makes the best thread, as it is strong and durable and fine enough for the purpose. Sew with a whipstitch in the manner used for the original stitching.

Timpani sticks should always be held so that the seam of the stitching is on the up side so as not to contact the drumhead, as the seam will produce an inferior tone. As an aid to keeping the sticks in the proper position, mark a line or cross in heavy pencil on the handle of the stick near the ball to indicate where the seam is located. This pencil mark should be visible to the player at all times to insure against striking the seams.

If the threaded end of the stick protrudes beyond the washer used to hold the beater ball or disc in place by more than a quarter inch or so, it should be sawed off. White marks, and even small tears, often are inflicted on the timpani head by an excess length of wood protruding beyond the ball.

PLAYING SPOT

The usual playing spot on the timpani head is shown in Figure 6.10.

Figure 6.10. Playing spots.

The playing spot should be located between an adjacent pair of tuning handles, in order to avoid entangling the sticks with the handles. Many newer models have either collapsible or removable tuning handles which avoids this problem altogether. When using calfskin heads, the exact spot on the surface of each head which sounds most resonant has to be determined by experimentation and is subject to a great deal of variation, changing from time to time even on the same head. This is generally not true of plastic heads and, of course, is a definite advantage of these heads. Some types of kettledrums cannot be rotated to bring this optimum playing area into position convenient for playing. This holds true for the Dresden type, some models of standard pedal timpani, and rotary timpani. Hand-tuned and most models of pedal timpani can be placed so that the optimum playing spot is in a good position. To produce the best sound, once this general good playing area has been located, the heads should be struck in an area not closer than two inches nor further than five inches from the rim. Played too close to the rim, a head will produce a "pinging" sound. As you approach the center, the deader the sound becomes. If struck in the center, there will be practically no vibration and the pitch will hardly be discernible.

SET-UPS FOR TWO, THREE AND FOUR KETTLES

The pair of timpani is placed so that the high (small) kettle is at the right of the low (large) one. The pedals are placed at an angle so that they can be easily reached by the R and L feet respectively. As the player stands or sits in playing position, no tuning handle should lie directly in the path to be traveled by either stick.

When three kettles are used it ordinarily will be most convenient to use one large and two small timpani, but there are exceptions to this. Place the kettle that sounds best on the extreme high tones on the right, the second small kettle in the center, and the large drum on the left. By arranging the three kettles in a semicircle, the pedals and playing surfaces can be kept within easy reach of the player.

When four timpani are needed, they should be arranged in the form of a half-circle in order to bring the pedals and the playing surfaces of all drums within reach of the timpanist. The kettles should be set close together, but not so close that one will actually contact another. Very often the four timpani available will not constitute a matched set. In this case, the two center drums should be the best of the four, as the bulk of the playing will likely be done on these inside kettles. The two outside drums, particularly if they are of the hand-tuned type, often can be preset to the highest and lowest tones of the composition and used for only these tones. This practice cannot always be followed, however, particularly in certain modern works which demand a large number of tuning changes throughout the entire register.

PLAYING POSITIONS

Most players prefer to stand while playing the timpani. The correct standing position is shown in Figures 6.14 and 6.15. Note that the player leans

Figure 6.11. Placement of the pair of timpani.

Figure 6.13. Placement of four timpani.

Figure 6.12. Placement of three timpani.

Figure 6.14. Playing position, front view.

Figure 6.15. Playing position, side view.

Figure 6.16. Seated playing position.

The types of kettledrums which are mounted on detachable tripods can be tilted to bring them into a position for either standing or sitting. However, these are rather obsolete models and are rapidly disappearing.

Figure 6.17. Timpani on tripods tilted for standing playing position.

Figure 6.18. Timpani on tripods, seated position.

somewhat forward. An erect standing position does not permit adequate leverage and balance. The taller the player the more he will have to lean forward to maintain this balance.

A timpani stool is required in certain situations, particularly when the part calls for two simultaneous changes of tuning necessitating the use of both feet on the pedals at the same time. In other compositions there may occur only sporadic single notes for the timpani, and a stool is a help in reducing the fatigue which comes from standing during long rests. Many timpanists play everything, or nearly everything, from a seated position. If a stool is used it should be high enough to bring the seat portion up to the same level as the rim of the kettledrums. Some players use a stool and play from a seated position in music which is not technically demanding, but leave the stool for a standing position which will permit better leverage when the going gets rough.

TIMPANI STICK HANDHOLDS

There are two contrasting schools of timpani technique each of which employs its own style of holding the sticks. It should be said, however, that there is a great deal of latitude within each of the two main schools. For convenience in referring to these two main styles we can designate them as "French" and "German," although to do so may not be entirely accurate. The German school holds its sticks "overhand," in the manner of the R snare drumstick. The forearm and wrist are held comparatively straight. The French style involves grasping the timpani stick with the thumb on top of the stick, fingers curled loosely around the underside. This method depends largely on suppleness of wrist and finger action. Soft volume rolls are made by alternately squeezing and releasing the fingers as they curl around the handle of the stick. A number of American players have adopted a style of holding the sticks and making the timpani stroke which is a cross between the two extremes. It is recommended that the beginning student learn the German handhold first, as this is used by a majority of players for most notes of moderate and loud volumes. The French handhold is useful when making a very soft roll, but this is a later refinement in technique which does not concern the beginner.

In teaching the German handhold the following stepwise procedure is recommended:

1. Grasp each stick at a point about ⅓ of the way up from the butt end with the thumb running parallel to the stick and opposed by the first joint of the forefinger. The strength of the grip on the stick is controlled almost entirely by the thumb and forefinger.

2. Curl the second, ring, and little fingers loosely around the stick. The little finger should not touch the wood. These fingers serve to guide the stick, and activate certain very small motions of the stick. They remain in light contact with the stick by opening up, or giving way, as the stick makes its backswing prior to a loud stroke.

3. Practice throwing the wrists forward and back while holding the sticks in the foregoing manner, simulating the action which will be used later to make the stroke on the timpani.

THE BASIC SINGLE STROKE

The first class or individual exercises for the timpani stroke can be done on practice pads or any

Figure 6.19. German handhold.

Figure 6.20. French handhold.

Figure 6.21. Backswing.

Figure 6.22. Start of downswing.

drumhead. It is not absolutely necessary to have the timpani to play on at first, although it would be desirable. Using the so-called German handhold, the first study should be the alternating of slow strokes. Both the R and the L work alike. Raise the arm in a relaxed manner, elbow first, followed by the wrist, and finally the hand. The ball of the stick should lag behind. This "up-phase" of the stroke is done slowly, but starting at the top of the downswing the velocity of the beater ball increases rapidly until it reaches its maximum speed and force at impact. Figures 6.21, 6.22 and 6.23 show the path of the arm, hand and stick in making a full stroke with the R. The L is identical, but reversed. The natural rebound from the timpani head should be absolutely free. Any continued downward pressure on the head will cause a muffling of the tone. *Tone* is ever the watchword in timpani playing! A useful concept is to think of *drawing the tone out of the drum* rather than pounding it in. Only by making a resilient stroke and allowing a free rebound of the sticks can this concept be realized.

It must be realized that the above procedure uses exaggerated and excessive motions in order to teach the concepts and movements involved to the beginning student. These motions must be refined

and considerably reduced as the student progresses. The wrist's snap-like action is the key to good timpani strokes whether they be loud or soft.

STICKWORK

The general rule for stickwork in timpani playing is: when alternating between the high and low drum, use the R on the high drum and the L on the low. In passages which stay on one or the other kettles, alternate sticking also may be used. In actual practice, however, there is a wide variation in the stickwork employed in similar situations by different players. Many timpanists prefer to use a great deal of repetition of the same stick when playing certain kinds of figures on one drum, for example, in a series of triplets at slow tempo, where all notes are of equal volume.

It is felt that a more even tone and volume production can be maintained in this manner. This approach is, perhaps, better left to the professional rather than the beginner. In rapid tempi also, doubling of sticks will be easier to execute than cross-sticking. For example:

The cross-sticking given in the foregoing example would be needlessly awkward. The timpanist occasionally will run across situations which demand that one stick be crossed over the other, but when there is an alternative it should be used.

The following examples illustrate recommended and alternate stickwork in a variety of typical timpani passages.

Figure 6.23. Impact.

R   R   R   L   R   L   R   R   L   L   L   R

(R   R   R   L)

3. Sietz' original stick indications are in parentheses in Study #2. Unless the tempo be very fast, the alternated sticking is just as good.

In D, A
(♩ = 108)

Sietz

4. The bracketed figures must be perceived as units to avoid cross-overs in Study #4.

In D, A
Slowly (♩ = 104)

Hochzeitmarch from Midsummer Nights Dream Music

5. In C, G

Mendelssohn

rit.

6. In C, F

Allegro

7. In A, E

Vivace

Beethoven

8. In E, B

Allegro

mf R R L R R   L L L R L   R   R L R L L L L R L R   LRL

R   R L R L   R L R L R L R L R   R   L R L R   L L L R L R   L L R L
(L R L R L   R)

RLR RLR R   L R   L R L L L R L L R L L L   R L R L   R L R L R   L R L

R   L R L R   L   R   L R L R   L R L R L   R L R L   L

DAMPING

The timpanist must know how to damp the ringing tone of the timpani which, if allowed to vibrate, will sustain for a surprisingly long time. Damping is done with the hand opposite the one which plays the note to be damped. A firm downward pressure near the center of the timpani head is required, as shown in Figure 6.24. A circular motion around the center of the head with the extended fingertips of the hand will also serve to damp the tone of the timpani.

Only on staccato, sharply accented, or *sfz* notes should the tone be damped very suddenly. Usually it is best to allow the tone to ring at least for the duration of the note's written value. In some cases the

Figure 6.25. Damping with same hand.

tone should be left to vibrate freely regardless of its written value, for example:

written:

Waltz

sounding:

This and similar passages require the timpanist to exercise his best musical judgment. Experience with a variety of literature is necessary to bring maturity

Figure 6.24. Damping with opposite hand.

of interpretation. A good policy for the beginning kettledrummer would be to damp:

1. those notes which seem to clash with the succeeding harmony;
2. those notes which precede general rests or pauses;
3. fermatas and final notes at the conductor's cut-off.

In fast moving passages when there is not time to damp with the opposite hand, an alternative is to damp with the hand which holds the stick. Contact the head with the tips of the fingers. Do not let any part of the stick touch the head. This method of damping is shown in Figure 6.25.

The word "coperto" (pl. "coperti") means to muffle the head of the kettledrum by covering a segment of it with a piece of soft cloth such as felt or baize. American scores usually use the indication "muffle" or "muffle with a cloth" to mean the same thing. The effect of such muffling is a deadening of the natural tone of the timpani. The piece of cloth should be placed on the head at a point opposite to the playing spot. The degree to which the tone is muffled is dependent upon the size and weight of the fabric used for the purpose, and where the fabric is placed (center, edge, etc.).

Figure 6.26. Timpani coperto.

THE TIMPANI ROLL

The timpani roll is produced by a rapid alternation of single strokes. In this respect it resembles the roll of the xylophone and marimba. The objective is to produce a steady tone, with a very minimum of stick sound (impact of beater-ball and head). The underlying physical principle of the timpani roll is: *the head is set in motion by the initial impact of the stick on the head, and then this vibration is reinforced at the same point in its vibrational path by succeeding*

impacts. Stated another way, the sticks' impacts must be *in phase* with the rate of vibration of the timpani head. From a practical standpoint, what this means is that the rate of roll alternation must be more rapid for high tones than for low ones. The steady and even flow of tone exemplified in the roll of the expert timpanist is made possible only by great care in the timing of the alternating strokes. If there is too rapid a rate of alternations a choked tone will result; with too slow a rate there will be "holes" in the sound.

Rolls on the kettledrum require a little accenting on the first stroke in order to establish the tone precisely on the beat. If the roll is tied over and/or ends *on* a beat, a definitive final stroke is also required. Both sticks must traverse equal arcs in order to produce sounds of equal volume. Arm, wrist, and hand muscles should be relaxed and supple. The concept to be kept uppermost in mind is "draw the tone out of the drum." A feeling of freedom of rebound goes hand in hand with the development of a feeling for proper roll speed. "Let the sticks do the work" is a useful idea in timpani playing as well as in snare drumming.

For rolls at *p* or *pp* volume, use the French handhold previously described. The alternating stick motions are activated by the squeezing and releasing of the fingers as they curl under the handles. See Figure 6.27. A lighter touch for very soft rolls is more possible through this method than is usually possible with the so-called German style, although individual preference may govern the eventual choice.

In the case of a crescendo roll, starting at *p* or *pp* level, the player can begin the roll with the thumb-on-top finger roll, and as the volume is increased switch gradually to the overhand (German) position. The latter is naturally a more powerful position and better adapted to loud playing.

Figure 6.27. Timpani roll, **pp** volume.

Figure 6.28. Timpani roll, **mf** volume.

Figure 6.29. Timpani, **f** volume.

In the decrescendo, it will be found somewhat awkward to switch from the overhand to the thumb-on-top handhold without perceptibly interrupting the flow of the alternations. The student should practice the decrescendo roll using the German position "all the way down."

Legato rolls are very common in timpani music. When a slur mark is used to connect rolls of different pitch, a special trick will help the player to effect a smooth connection when moving from one kettle to another, as in the figure:

The trick is simply to move one stick to the next kettle on the beat while the other stick remains to finish out the tone. The lead stick, when moving from the high to the low drum, will be the L. When moving from the low to the high kettle the R stick goes first. The lead stick starts the tone with its initial blow and thus gives the illusion that the roll has already begun, when actually it takes about half a second before the second stick can be brought into position and the true alternations of the roll begin. Legato rolls are encountered so often in timpani parts that it will repay the student to master the technique just described through careful practice.

Another roll commonly found in timpani parts is the forte-piano (fp) roll such as:

This is so often played incorrectly and it is a very simple matter to execute properly. The secret is to let the drum do the work for you. Don't fight it as so many timpanists do. To produce this roll properly, strike the drum with a strong stroke. Permit the vibrations created to die away until the sound reaches the degree of softness desired. When this point is reached, resume rolling again to maintain the desired level of softness (or gradually crescend as in example two above).

TUNING THE TIMPANI

It can be stated without fear of contradiction that tuning is the most difficult aspect of timpani playing. No matter what type of kettledrum is used, securing good intonation will be the timpanist's major problem. Several factors are involved. First of all, the kettledrum tone is not a pure tone, but a complex one from an acoustical standpoint. The complexity of the overtone structure varies from one kettle to another, from one point to another on the surface of one head, and from low to high notes on the same kettle. Differences in thickness, soft spots, and textural dissimilarities in the head are partly responsible for these variations. A second difficulty lies in the ease with which timpani heads vibrate sympathetically to a variety of frequencies. Notes which sound in tune to the timpanist when played with the other instruments often sound out of tune on a solo entrance. Another factor, probably unrecognized in most cases, is the acoustical property of the stage, hall or rehearsal room. Sometimes a place which is "dead" acoustically will make accurate tuning all but impossible, to the great consternation of the timpanist. The resonance of timpani bowls is another factor, since some notes will be more easily obtainable than others due to the shape of the bowls. Under certain conditions a needed note may seem to lie at a particularly nonresonant point in the timpani's range, and will therefore be difficult to tune accurately.

The one general principle for tuning any timpani is: *the tension must be kept equal at all points around the perimeter of the head if a clear tone is to result.*

The student will require some reference device to obtain his pitch unless he happens to be blessed with absolute pitch. A circular pitch pipe is recommended for the beginner, although the one or two octave translations are somewhat of a problem to some students. For students who have well-developed relative pitch, an A 440 tuning fork is all that should be necessary. General musicianship studies such as melodic and harmonic dictation, solfeggio, and related studies are requisite for the high school and college timpanist who expects to develop himself fully. For young students, the most practical method of objectifying pitch relationships is the use of the sol-fa syllables. Unfortunately for many young percussionists, the elementary school music curriculum does not include the learning of syllables in many districts at present. The instructor in this case will probably find that time spent at the beginning of tuning study in learning the rudiments of syllable singing will be time well spent, for without some groundwork in pitch relationships most beginners will find timpani tuning completely impossible. The relation of *do* to *sol*, and *fa* to *do* must be established in the first stages of timpani tuning study. All of the intervals must eventually be mastered.

Before any timpani head can be played upon it must be put in tune with itself, i.e., it must be tensioned so that it produces the same frequency of vibration at each point around its perimeter. All types of kettledrums have handles or keys by which tension can be applied to the counterhoop, and it is by means of these handles or keys that the head can be put into tune with itself. Hand-tuned drums have no additional means of regulating the tension. When making this preliminary tuning, adjust the handles to bring their areas of the head to the pitch of the portion selected as the playing spot.

The best way to test the tuning at each handle is to flick the middle fingertip sharply on the timpani head to set up a vibration which can be heard at close range, but is unaudible a distance away. There is a knack to listening for the fundamental tone of the timpani. At the moment of impact many overtones will be heard. The true fundamental isolates itself from the aggregate sound as a "ringing" tone *slightly after* the moment of impact. The player must

crouch over to bring his ear close to the edge of the timpani head to hear the ring that is made by the finger-flick. See Figure 6.30. For beginners, it is recommended that they first hum the pitch to themselves before matching it on the drum.

Figure 6.30. Timpanist in position to test tuning.

If hand-tuned timpani are available it is recommended that tuning study begin on them. To prepare the hand-tuned timpani for playing, tune the low drum to A and the high drum to *d* . The usual procedure is to grasp a pair of handles at once, one with each hand in the following order:

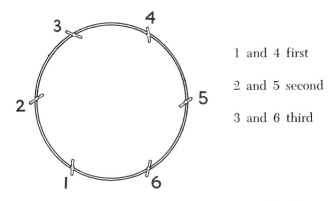

Figure 6.31. Diagram of numbered tuning handles.

1 and 4 first

2 and 5 second

3 and 6 third

Practice will show the approximate amount of turn needed at each handle to tune the various intervals. It is a good plan to try to tune rapidly enough so that the ring which results from the finger-flick can be heard rising or falling in pitch.

To settle the head after tuning, make a quick circular motion around the drumhead with the hand, using a downward pressure. This will tend to lower the pitch a little but will prevent the head from going flat while it is being played upon. To compensate for this flatting, tune slightly sharp before settling the head.

The essential feature of all pedal tuning devices is that a downward pressure of the toe on the foot pedal *raises* the pitch, and an upward movement (toe up—heel down) of the pedal causes the head to slacken and thus *lowers* the pitch. To prepare the pedal timpani for playing, the heads of both kettles should be set at their extreme low notes. For the 28″ kettle, release the pedal pressure by putting the heel to its lowest position. Now tune the head to the low *F* by means of the tuning handles. This creates the proper amount of tension on the head, enabling it to sound its best throughout its range. The tone of the timpani will not be full and resonant unless great care is taken to tune the extreme low notes accurately preparatory to the rehearsal or performance. The 25″ kettle is set at its low note, *Bb*, by the method just described.

The pedal-tuning operation is somewhat simpler than hand-tuning in that the three tuning steps are accomplished with one movement of the foot pedal. Otherwise, however, the techniques are the same. The player must set the head ringing by the finger-flick, listen at a point near the head, and arrest the foot motion at the instant the pitch of the timpani's ring has reached the new pitch. It is usually easier to approach the new note from below when tuning with the pedal, in the manner of the string player's tuning procedure.

Rotary timpani are tuned by turning the bowls clockwise to raise the pitch and counterclockwise to lower it. Grasp one or two of the tuning handles to turn the kettle. Notes at the upper end of the register require quite a lot of torsion to be exerted because of the resistance of the taut head, so the kettle sometimes must be steadied while turning. Familiarity with a particular set of rotary timpani enables the player to learn the approximate amount of turn needed to tune the various intervals. One model, recommended for school use, has a pointer and preset tabs around the edge of the counterhoop to indicate where to stop the rotation for each note. This model is shown in Figure 6.5.

As a guide to instruction in beginning the study of timpani tuning, there follows a set of stepwise procedures for making each tuning change.

1. Set starting note.
2. Play until tuning change indicated. Damp last note.

3. To change note, flick head with finger, ear close to timpani.
4. Hum, or think, next note.
5. Turn handles, adjust pedal, or rotate bowl until new note is reached. Tune slightly sharp.
6. Settle head.
7. Play new note.
8. Check accuracy of tuning; adjust if necessary.

Take time to tune each interval accurately at first. Students should practice with the aim of cutting down the time needed to accomplish the foregoing steps. Most good method books for the timpani devote a number of exercises to the problem of making tuning changes. In these studies, as well as in most actual music, the direction to change note will occur during a long rest. See example below:

In such an actual musical context the player must maintain the count while at the same time accomplishing the steps of his tuning change. Needless to say, this demands a real power of concentration.

A mechanical aid to timpani tuning has been on the market for a number of years. The so-called *tuning gauges* attach to the inner sides of the timpani bowls, and consist of rods which move up and down with the action of the pedals and pivoted indicators activated by the pedal motions which point to preset note tabs. A pair are shown in Figure 6.3. Although not prohibitively expensive (about $50.00 a pair at current prices), these gauges are not recommended for use with calfskin timpani heads because they are too inaccurate. Once set to the pedal tuning of low *F* for the large drum, for example, then any variation in atmospheric conditions would throw off all the readings on the gauge. Any experienced timpanist will vouch for the fact that these changes do occur, and often suddenly, as in an auditorium where ventilation is accomplished by opening of stage doors, side doors, etc. Air conditioned halls, theaters, and auditoriums are likewise subject to minute-by-minute fluctuations in the relative humidity. Tuning gauges could be an aid in tuning timpani equipped with weatherproof plastic heads. They could be very useful for training young players as well as for saving time for the instructor, but it should always be borne in mind that the final arbiter is the *ear*. Students using timpani with tuning gauges should be taught not to depend completely upon the readings of the gauges, but to *listen* at all times. The speed at which the pedal is raised or lowered, or the bowl rotated, can affect the accuracy with which the gauge measures the tension on the head. Gauges can be of some use to the timpanist in coping with the problem of making many rapid tuning changes in a limited amount of time, where approximate accuracy would be superior to guesswork. It is chiefly in such emergency situations that the tuning gauges are used by professional timpanists.

NOTATION

Timpani music is written in the F clef, sounding as written. The one exception occurs in some editions of certain Baroque and early Classic works, where the early custom of writing all timpani parts for the tonic and dominant notes as *C* and *G* is still followed. In each such case the actual pitches are clearly specified at the beginning of the first line of music.

Most timpani parts specify the starting notes for each kettledrum at the top of the page and/or the beginning of the first line. There is no standard order, however, and this can be confusing. A helpful aid is the staff with the actual pitches clearly shown.

If such an indication is not printed on the page, it is a simple matter to draw one in in pencil at the top of the page. If succeeding movements of a composition require different settings, these should be pencilled in at the start of each movement.

Abbreviations for the timpani are: timp., tym., tymp., tymps., tp. The word *kettledrum* may be used interchangeably for *timpani*. For the foreign equivalents, see the table of foreign language percussion terms in Chapter 2.

Rolls for the timpani are indicated by three slanted dashes through the note stem: . The final note of a tied-over roll is the concluding sound of that roll: . A timpani roll is usually ended with the same stick used to begin it. One slanted dash through a note stem means to divide that note into eighth notes; two slanted dashes—sixteenth notes. In some classic scores three dashes must be interpreted as thirty-second notes, *not* a roll. The famous passage from Beethoven's *Ninth Symphony* quoted is an example at the bottom of the page.

In older music rolls are often indicated by means of the trill sign:

Grace notes are not uncommon in timpani writing. When they are encountered they should be played with single sticking:

Tremolos between two tones are indicated thus:

In this case the roll is simply split between the two kettles.

Notation of glissandi should be properly understood.

In example one above, the F is struck and the pedal depressed until the B♭ is reached and then the head is damped. If the glissando is notated as in the second example above, the F is struck and the pedal is depressed. When the B♭ is reached, it is also struck and then the head is damped. In other words, if the note on which the glissando concludes is a grace note, only the first note is struck; however, if both the first and last notes are written as full value notes, then both get a separate attack.

TRICKS OF THE TIMPANIST'S TRADE

When it is necessary to change the tuning of one or more timpani during the course of a composition, it is a great help if the new note or notes can be picked out from the general sound to serve as cues. These cues can then be pencilled into the part at the points during rests and tacet portions of the piece.

In tonal music it is usually possible to get adequate cues to insure that the drums can be kept in good tune. In compositions where the tonality shifts rapidly or in atonal compositions, the timpanist will be on his own, so to speak, and must use any and every aid available as pitch reference.

An "ear" for timpani tuning can be trained, but the novice can be easily discouraged by the slow rate of progress. Listening intently to the progressions of harmony and melody at all times is the best way to develop the ear. As has been mentioned, the formal study of solfeggio, with copious amounts of dictation, is a great help in training the timpanist to tune accurately. Even such relatively simple devices as memorizing the sound of intervals by identifying them in familiar tunes is a real help. Use of the sol-fa syllables has also been mentioned as a useful device. For the beginner, the first step in ear training is to match tones with the singing voice or hum tone. A piano or other bass register instrument can be utilized to sound the tones, which can first be matched by the voice, later by the timpani following the procedure of tuning.

It is very helpful to the timpanist to be able to think, hum, or sing a reliable *A* at any time. Practice with an *A* fork or pitch pipe should be started early and continued until the student can remember the sound and reproduce it at any time. Some students will experience great difficulty in learning to do this, others will find it quite easy. One aid for the orchestra timpanist is to associate the memory of *A* with the sound of the open *A* as it predominates when string instruments tune up. From *A*, the next most useful note is probably small *d*, a fourth above.

It will often be found useful to preset the outer kettle, or kettles, when more than a pair are used, to the extremes of the range required in a given composition. Thus, if the lowest note needed is *E* and the highest *g*, the timpanist should tune the lowest kettle (extreme L) to sound *E* when its pedal is in heel-down position, and the highest kettle (extreme R) to sound *g* when the pedal is in toe-down position. He will then be reasonably close to these notes when the pedals are moved back to these positions, should they have to be changed during intervening parts of the composition.

The placement of the timpani in the symphony orchestra has not been the subject of serious acoustical study. Expediency is usually the criterion for placement. The author would tend to agree with White, who advocates that the timpani be placed near the trumpets and French horns. In music of the Baroque, Classical, and to some extent the Romantic periods, the kettledrums formed a sort of bass register to brass parts. The timpani, even in more modern works, often enter with the brasses, and many of their rhythmic figures are identical. For this reason alone the idea of placing the kettledrums alongside, or directly behind, the brasses merits consideration. The timpani should *not* be placed next to the bass drum, as the large heads of each tend to pick up much unwanted sound through sympathetic vibration.

Round fibre or wooden covers should be kept over the heads of the timpani when they are not in use. If a four-kettle set-up is employed and the composition being played requires that only the two inner kettles be used, leave the fibre head covers *on* the outer drums to keep their heads from ringing sympathetically.

When the school music instructor identifies a student as showing aptitude and probable talent for timpani playing, he should lose no time in placing the student under the guidance of the best private timpani instructor in the area. The mastery of these demanding instruments is a lifetime of study and entails in nearly every case serious private study with an expert teacher.

CHAPTER 7

Other Percussion Instruments

THE TRIANGLE

The triangle is the most frequently used of the small percussion instruments often referred to as "traps." It is an ancient instrument, often depicted in early Renaissance paintings being played by angels and members of heavenly choirs. These paintings usually show the triangle as having three or more circular jingles attached to the lower leg of the triangle. This early form of the triangle was known as a *cymbale*, and represented an intermediate step in the development of the triangle from its ancestor, the *sistrum*, an instrument developed in ancient Egypt consisting of a frame with handle and thin metal rods which would rattle when the instrument was shaken. The triangle in its present form came into use in the orchestra in the early years of the eighteenth century. Both Haydn and Mozart scored for the triangle, and both employed the instrument to lend a Near-Eastern coloration to certain passages. The bass drum, cymbals and triangle were adopted into the orchestra originally to obtain the effects of the Turkish music which was having considerable influence on European composers of the eighteenth century.

Much tonal variation is possible from the triangle, and is dependent upon the weight of the beater used, the spot struck, and the kind of stroke. Each triangle has its own distinctive set of frequencies, which consist of clashing upper partials of the unheard fundamental. The best triangle tone does not exhibit any definite pitch, but only a shimmering metallic quality which has considerable brilliance. The tone of a triangle has the ability to cut through the total orchestral texture, even when played very softly.

Triangles are made in a variety of sizes, from tiny 3″ models to the 12″ to 14″ large sizes. Their diameters may vary from about 1/4″ to 1/2″, the 7/16th″

Figure 7.1. Triangle.

diameter being the most popular for smaller triangles. Plated steel is used for both the triangle and the beater.

In school bands and orchestras where one triangle must do general duty the recommended size is the 8″ model. This triangle is large enough to produce the heavier tones when needed, yet light tones are possible by the use of light beaters and light strokes. The symphony orchestra percussion equipment should include a 6″ and a 10″ triangle in addition to one or more around 8″ in size. When selecting triangles the purchaser should be governed more by the sounds obtainable than mere dimensions.

The standard triangle beater is a steel rod with a loop at one end for convenience in holding. It can also be hung from this loop. The weights vary, and two or three different weights should be available to the player. Experimentation will show which sizes work best for a particular triangle. The triangle will not sound good if it is struck with wood, such as a snare drumstick. However, this is called for sometimes, as a special effect.

An extremely important item is a good device for holding the triangle. The commercial holder consists of a metal clamp which attaches to the music stand and has a loop of gut from which to suspend the triangle so that it will be at the correct angle for easy playing. Unless a very thin gut string is used, there will be considerable deadening of the tone. A discarded violin gut *D* or *G* string is right for the purpose. A very satisfactory triangle holder can be made from a wooden clothes pin, or the clamp section of the clip used to keep music from blowing off music stands. See Figure 7.1. Drill two small holes about an inch apart in the underside of the clothes pin or clip to accommodate the loop of gut. Secure a piece of gut string to form a loop which will suspend the triangle about one inch below the clamp. The advantage of such a holder is that it can be removed from its place on the music rack and replaced after playing easily and quickly.

Another useful type of triangle holder can be made from the base section of the common collapsible music stand. A metal rod of the same diameter as the upper section of the music stand, three to four feet long and bent to a right angle at the top, forms the upper section for this handy type of holder. Two holes must be drilled near the end of the angled rod through which the gut loop can pass. The great advantage of the floor stand triangle holder is that it permits the player to use two beaters, yet still maintains the triangle in a position which is both convenient and high enough so that the tone will carry.

When the triangle is played it should be held up in front of the player about chest high. Only in emergency, when there is not time to take the triangle off the music stand, should the triangle be left clamped to the stand. The tone of the triangle will project well if it is unimpeded by music stands and the backs of seated musicians. Figure 7.2 shows the best method of holding the triangle in playing position.

Notation for the triangle varies considerably. In composite scoring, where snare drum, bass drum, cymbals, triangle, etc., are all printed on one or two staves, the triangle notes are usually placed on the upper line or in the upper space of the top staff. In most cases notes to be played on the triangle will be clearly marked *triangle*, *tri.*, or *trgl.* Sometimes the noteheads will be x-shaped to set them off from snare drum notes on the same staff. If a tie or slur mark extends after a triangle note, allow the tone to ring.

Figure 7.2. Triangle playing position.

Staccato dots are often used to indicate that the tone of the triangle should be damped quickly. Rolls are indicated by three slanted dashes through the note stem or under or over whole notes, or by the trill sign.

The usual playing spot is the outside of the right leg of the triangle, but triangles vary in this respect, and the player must determine by experimentation the optimum playing spot for the particular triangle. There is no rule or custom to prohibit the use of any spot on the triangle if it produces a good tone. Assuming that the triangle is held in the left hand and played with the right, then the most convenient playing surfaces would be the inside of the lower leg and the outside of the right leg.

A light wrist motion should be used in striking the triangle. The tone should be drawn out of the instrument. The sound to avoid is a clang which sounds like a dinner bell, or a roll which sounds like a fire gong. Such poor tones from triangles are all too common, and are due to using too heavy a beater, too heavy a stroke, or both.

Damping is possible by the R finger tips or can be done with the fingers of the L hand while holding the clamp. A light contact of the fingertips is sufficient to stop the tone.

The triangle roll is produced either by a series of quick wrist motions with the beater held close to a corner of the triangle or by the use of two beaters on the outside legs of the instrument. The upper corner is easier, as the beater is not working against gravity as it would be in one of the lower corners. The wrist shake must be well controlled so that the force of the alternating contacts of the beater with the legs of the triangle will be equal. The single strokes will produce a good sounding roll if they are rapidly executed. See Figure 7.3. In the two-beater method, a certain disadvantage lies in the fact that the triangle will have to remain clamped to the music stand and cannot be brought up to its best playing position. See Figure 7.4. In such a situation the floor stand triangle holder would solve the problem.

Figure 7.3. Triangle roll.

Figure 7.4. Triangle roll, two beaters.

THE TAMBOURINE

The tambourine is a hybrid instrument, being a membrane covered frame drum with metal jingles. Like the triangle, it is an ancient instrument and is thought to have evolved from the sistrum. Modern tambourines consist of a circular maple shell with apertures cut at equidistant points through which pins are mounted to hold the tiny pairs of nickel-played cymbals, called jingles. One side is covered with a calfskin head, tacked down tautly, and shellacked to make it somewhat impervious to weather conditions. Some tambourines have a double set of jingles mounted on each pin. Diameters vary from 6″ to 10″. Tambourines with plastic heads and head tensioning mechanisms are available also.

Figure 7.5. Tambourine.

A good quality 10″ tambourine with either single or double jingles is recommended for school use when one tambourine is to do general duty. Most of the cheap imported tambourines have flimsy shells which warp or crack easily and heads of inferior quality.

There is no particularly standard way of notating tambourine music. When the percussion parts are printed on one or two staves, the tambourine notes are usually placed on a line or space above the snare drum part. In any case, the notes to be played by the tambourine are clearly indicated by the word *tambourine, tamb., tam.,* at the beginning of the line of music, or at such places as the tambourine enters. Some of the common foreign equivalents for *tambourine* are: *tambour de basque,* (Fr.); *tamburino, tamburo basco*, (It.); *beckentrommel*, (Ger.); and *tambuorin*, (Ger.).

To hold the tambourine, grasp the open side of the shell just over the small hole drilled in the shell with the fingers of the left hand. Place the L thumb on the outside of the shell and parallel with the head. Do not put the thumb or a finger in the hole on the side of the shell. For a playing position which will best project the sound to the audience, hold the instrument at almost face level (not above eye level). So many tambourine players, as well as players of the other miscellaneous hand held percussion instruments, insist on playing these instruments at a low, almost subterranean level. Visually and audibly this is poor positioning. Projection to the audience is most important. See Figure 7.6.

Figure 7.6. Usual playing position and stroke.

There are at least four types of strokes used for executing single strokes on the tambourine.

1. The usual stroke for medium to loud notes is made by forming the fingers and thumb of the R hand into a small tight "ball" of flesh and bringing this sharply into contact with the tambourine head, using a sharp wrist action. See Figure 7.6. It is best to hold the tambourine practically stationary and move the R hand, because to do the reverse will produce many extra jingle sounds as the tambourine is moved. There must be resiliency to the stroke. *Exception*: when the tone must be damped suddenly, the hand should remain in contact with the tambourine and held firmly there for a second or two until the jingles have stopped vibrating.

2. For notes of soft volume, hold the tambourine as in (1), but instead of striking the tambourine with the "ball" of flesh formed by the fingers and thumb, tap the head near the edge with the tips of the first three fingers. See Figure 7.7. A variation of the foregoing stroke, used when very soft notes are needed, is to contact the tambourine head with the heel of the playing hand and tap lightly with the finger tips. This muffles the resonance of the tambourine and aids in controlling the volume. The tambourine solo in the *Danse Arabe* of Tschaikowsky's *Nutcracker Suite* traditionally is played in this manner.

3. When the tambourine part contains rhythm figures which are too rapid to execute with a single hand, the tambourine may be placed head side down on the knee, which has been raised by placing the foot on a chair or stool. In this position it is possible to use both hands to play the rhythm pattern.

Figure 7.7. Finger-tip stroke.

Figure 7.8. Knee position.

Rap the frame of the tambourine with the extended fingers of each hand, in the manner of the bongo player. The instrument is held secure by the weight of the forearms as they rest on its near edge.

A variant of the foregoing method is to place the tambourine head down on the trap table. The tone in this case will be somewhat muffled, but for soft passages it is quite satisfactory.

4. For parts which call for loud volume and rapid strokes, use the raised knee position, grasp the tambourine firmly, and strike the tambourine down on the knee and up against the R hand on alternate notes. Figure 7.9 shows the correct position.

There are two standard roll techniques. For long and/or loud rolls, hold the tambourine in the standard manner, but with the arm straight up, and rotate the

Figure 7.9. Knee and hand position.

Figure 7.10. Tambourine roll.

Figure 7.11. Tambourine thumb roll.

wrist as rapidly as possible. If this rotary motion is rapid and well controlled a very satisfactory roll will result. It is the only way to sustain a long trilled note. End the shake with a light tap of the R.

The second method produces a true roll by opposing the extended R thumb tip in a counterclockwise rotary motion around the perimeter of the head near the shell. The thumb works "against the grain," and thus causes a series of fine vibrations which are useful in playing a short and/or soft note which calls for a trill or roll. Moisten the thumb tip with saliva in order to cause enough friction to set up the vibration. Start rotating from the bottom near the L handhold and work up and around as far as it is possible to go, keeping the thumb always at the same angle to the head. The L handhold must be quite firm. As an aid in securing enough friction, some percussionists apply powdered rosin to the outer surface of the tambourine head. It must be applied often, usually before each playing period. Others glue double -O sandpaper around the outer edges of the tambourine head. Probably the best insurance for the thumb roll is to rub the thumb on a cake of the sticking agent used by bank tellers and secretaries. It can be procured at a stationery shop for a few cents a cake.

One of the hazards of tambourine playing is the tendency of the instrument to sound unwanted jingle noises when it is picked up preparatory to its entrance, or when replacing it on the trap table after use. Always keep the instrument flat when moving it to minimize extraneous jingle sounds.

THE TAM-TAM (GONG)

The tam-tam, or gong, is of ancient Oriental origin, and until rather recent times was reserved for musical passages with exotic flavor, as in "Orientales" and other descriptive forms. Modern composers use the tam-tam more for the sake of its inherent power to cap a climax or give an electric quality to the orchestral timbre than for any Oriental connotations.

The terms *gong* and *tam-tam* mean the same thing, at least in modern usage. Originally the word tam-tam was derived from an African word meaning simply *drum* (no doubt the same word from which we have derived *tom-tom*). Technically, a gong is a metal plate which emits a definite pitch, but such instruments are rarely used in Western music. The term gong has now become attached to the instrument of indefinite pitch

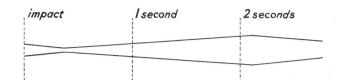

Figure 7.13. Diagram of tam-tam sound showing relationship of time and volume.

Its after-ring, in the case of a large gong of good quality, is extremely long in duration. The amplitude of vibration at the center of the instrument is wide, particularly when it is struck a heavy blow.

Small gongs do not have the crashy tone and long sustentation characteristic of the larger sizes. Some of the best gongs are imported from southeast Asia and are now distributed by leading percussion instrument manufacturers. The Paiste Company is producing beautiful, quality tam-tams and/or gongs. The most popular diameters are 24″, 26″, 28″, 30″, and 32″. For young school orchestras and bands the smaller of these sizes is adequate, but for high school, college and professional use a gong at least 28″ in diameter is recommended. Like cymbals, gongs are very expensive, selling at list prices of $90.00 to $230 for the sizes just mentioned. A heavy gong stand of pipe or tubular steel is required to hold the gong steady. One type consists of a wide base with a single supporting upright on which is mounted a circular frame within which the gong hangs. This type is adequate for the lighter weight tam-tams. The best type for suspending a heavy gong is a three-quarter circular frame supported by two feet which run at right angles to the instrument itself. Such a stand is shown in Figure 7.12.

The tone of a tam-tam is very dependent upon the beater used to strike it. A common type of commercial tam-tam beater has a rather heavy metal handle and a beater ball covered with lamb's wool. The center core of the tam-tam beater is usually weighted with lead in order to give it sufficient weight to bring out the full tone of the instrument. The larger the gong the heavier the beater must be. In addition to the lamb's wool previously mentioned, several kinds of material are used to cover gong beaters. Soft chamois, layers of wool cloth, and felt are often used. For rolls on the tam-tam two beaters somewhat smaller than the beater used for single notes are needed. A pair of bass drum beaters will usually suffice for the purpose, especially if they are wrapped beforehand with a layer of thick felt.

Figure 7.12. Tam-tam.

which is also called the tam-tam. It should be pointed out that some scores call for "tuned gongs" and will list the desired notes. Very few organizations have such instruments and, normally, these have to be rented. The term "tuned gong" is proper when referring to these type instruments. The term "tuned tam-tam" is never proper. Conductors and percussionists must be careful to distinguish between *tam-tam* and *tom-tom,* two very unlike instruments with similar names.

The tam-tam is one of the slowest speaking of the instruments. Its sound, when struck a sharp blow, does not appear to reach maximum intensity until a second or two after the blow.

Notation for the tam-tam is not standardized. Because the instrument is used sparingly in most compositions which call for it, the composer or arranger usually labels each note *gong, tam-tam,* or *T.T.* The notes usually appear on the lower lines or spaces of the F clef. Occasionally a special kind of notehead, such as a diamond-shape or an x, is used to indicate gong notes. A slur or tie after a note for the gong means to let the instrument ring beyond its written value at the discretion of the player. The direction "let ring" (in French—"laissez vibré") means to allow the tone to sustain without any damping whatsoever.

The point at which a tam-tam is struck influences the high and low partials that are included in the overall sound-range. A tam-tam struck dead center will produce a deep, sustained sound with the lower partials more predominant. Struck near the edge, a tam-tam sounds more high toned, bright, and "rustling." The higher partials sound out. The optimum playing spot to produce a deep, rich sound, rising gradually, and incorporating the full range of highs and lows is an area found slightly above, below, or to the side of the center. The percussionist must experiment under a variety of playing conditions and with a variety of beaters to determine the best playing spot on a particular tam-tam.

The stroke on the tam-tam is much like that used for the bass drum. The beater is grasped in the same manner as the bass drum's, with the thumb on top of the handle. For very light strokes only the wrist is needed, but for most gong tones the forearm is also brought into play. The concept of drawing the tone out of the instrument is particularly applicable in the case of the tam-tam. The player must be thoroughly familiar with his instrument in order to know how much force to use to obtain the various volume levels. A small variation in the force of the blow may result in a big difference in volume.

If there is opportunity to do so, the gong should be "warmed up" just before its entrance by brushing it lightly with the beater to start the vibration in advance of the actual note. This warming-up makes volume control a bit easier and also tends to cause the gong to speak more quickly after the impact.

The tam-tam roll is made with two beaters held in the manner of the two beaters used in the bass drum roll. Single strokes are alternated, more slowly than in the bass drum roll.

The tam-tam can be damped gradually or suddenly, depending upon the musical context. To damp the gong gradually, run the hand opposite to the beater hand slowly across the back surface of the gong. If the note to be damped in this manner is very loud, both hands will be required, one brushing against the back and one against the front. To damp the gong suddenly, press both hands against the front and back of the instrument at its center. To damp very loud crashes suddenly, one or both knees can be utilized to contact the vibrating gong. Figure 7.15 shows the gong being damped in the ordinary manner. Figure 7.16 illustrates the manner of damping with the knees.

Figure 7.14. Impact of the tam-tam stroke.

Figure 7.15. Damping the tam-tam with the hands.

Figure 7.16. Damping the tam-tam with the knees.

Figure 7.17. Woodblock played with xylophone stick.

THE WOODBLOCK

The woodblock is another of the small percussion instruments to be adopted into Western music from its original oriental usage in ritual and ceremonial music. During the early part of the jazz era in America the woodblock became associated with ragtime and Dixieland drumming. It is sometimes used to create a synthetic ragtime, soft-shoe, or Dixieland effect. In concert music it is used in a variety of ways, sometimes simply to provide a hollow wood sound as a contrast to the drums and the metal sounds of cymbals, triangle, or bells.

A good woodblock for general purposes would be one about 8″ x 2 1/2″ x 3″. This block will have one high pitched side and one lower in pitch, the difference in pitch resulting from a difference in width and location of the slotting. A block of this size can produce a heavy "bonk" and is also capable of making the lighter tap sounds.

The woodblock may be held in the L hand and struck with the R, using a xylophone mallet or snare drumstick. If rapid figures are called for the block can be placed on the trap table and played upon with two sticks.

Figure 7.18. Woodblock played with snare drumsticks.

Figure 7.19. Woodblock roll.

Two kinds of tone are obtainable and the choice of tone is a point of musical judgment. The heavy "bonk" sound is good for single notes where medium or loud volume is indicated. It is produced by striking the block on its top surface with the shoulder or butt end of a snare drumstick in such a manner that the maximum wood-against-wood contact is made. For a very heavy sound use hard rubber xylophone mallets. To produce light tapping "ticky" tones, play on the top of the block with the tips of the drumsticks. The sticks may be held with snare drum handholds, or both may be held as the R snare stick is held. The latter is usually more convenient when the block is placed on a rather low table.

A roll is possible on the woodblock, although it is seldom called for in band or orchestra music. The double-stroke snare drum roll is used, with the stick tips playing on the top surface of the block. See Figure 7.19.

Figure 7.21. Ordinary playing position for castanets.

Figure 7.20. Castanets.

THE CASTANETS

The castanets are of Spanish origin and are used in band and orchestra music when the composer wishes to impart a Spanish flavor to a piece such as a tango or other dance. The authentic castanets played by the Spanish dancers are pairs of shell-like wooden clappers, held by means of cords which are passed over the thumbs and dangled rather loosely in the palms of the hands. The rhythms are tapped with the four fingers on the outer shells which then contact the inner shells with a resonant "clack." To play castanets in this manner is an art. By way of making it easier for percussionists to play castanet rhythms, the castanet shells are mounted opposite one another, separated by a broad wooden handle. When the handle is shaken the castanets clap against the upper portion of the wood handle. One or two pairs of castanets can be mounted on a single handle.

The castanets are held in front of the player about chest high, with the handle at right angles to the floor. To sound the castanets, shake the handle back and forth so that the shells will alternate to sound the desired rhythm pattern. The L hand is held behind the castanets to assist in control and in readiness to damp at the end of the pattern, or on the cut-off. See Figure 7.21.

Another style of castanet playing is sometimes used, especially in loud passages, wherein the castanets are struck against the raised knee on the downstroke and against the cupped L hand on the upstroke. Precise rhythms are difficult to execute in this manner.

Figure 7.22. Knee and hand method for rapid castanet playing.

The chief difficulty in castanet playing lies in shaking the handle in exactly the right way to sound the desired rhythm. This is not at all easy to do because the loosely mounted shells are very prone to sound extra clacks before, during, and after the playing of the notated rhythm pattern. An excellent device, for making clean and precise castanet playing possible is in wide usage nowadays. It consists of a single castanet shell, or pair of shells, mounted on a resonant block of wood and held at an angle to this block by means of a spring. The player has merely to tap out the desired rhythm with a pair of snare drumsticks, xylophone mallets, or his fingers on the top of the castanet. A spring causes the castanet to snap up instantly to position for the next note. The sound compares very favorably with the authentic paired castanet arrangement. See Figure 7.23.

Figure 7.23. Spring-mounted type of castanets.

Castanet music is usually notated on one of the upper lines or spaces of the F clef, or on a single line running above or below the staff. In any case the part will be clearly marked *castanets, cast.* or *casts.*

When a roll is indicated for the castanets the handle is shaken back and forth as rapidly as possible, as shown in Figure 7.24. If the spring-mounted type of castanets are used, the correct roll for them is made by rapid single strokes of the drumsticks, mallets, or fingers.

TEMPLE BLOCKS

The temple blocks come from the Orient, where they are still used in Chinese temple ceremonies. The usual set consists of five blocks, each with a different pitch. The pitches are indefinite, but unmistakably "higher" or "lower." See the table of percussion instruments, Chapter 2, for a picture of the temple blocks. The set of blocks is mounted on a frame

Figure 7.24. Castanet roll.

with the lower pitched blocks to the left. They may be struck with xylophone mallets, felt timpani sticks, or snare drumsticks. Until very recently composers and arrangers wrote for the temple blocks only to suggest an Oriental atmosphere or as horsehoof imitations. At present the temple blocks are being employed to a greater degree for their own inherent sound, which is more mellow and mysterious than the ordinary woodblock, by many eminent composers.

RATCHET

This curious sound effect has been used by many composers in a variety of idioms. Richard Strauss, Offenbach, and Honneger (*Jeanne d' Arc*) have scored for the ratchet. See the table of percussion instruments, Chapter 2, for a picture of the ratchet. The instrument consists of two tongues of wood which are made to vibrate when a notched cylinder is cranked. The chattering sound made by the ratchet has no clear associative or imitative qualities. The ordinary manner of playing the ratchet is to attach it by means of a clamp to the hoop of a bass drum or edge of a trap table. To sound the ratchet, the handle is turned clockwise. It is necessary to turn the handle at a constant rate of speed in order to maintain a steady volume of sound.

SLAPSTICK

The slapstick and the whip-crack are essentially alike. Figure 7.25 illustrates the type which is activated by a whip-cracking motion. Another type is

Figure 7.25. Whip-crack.

Figure 7.26. Slapstick.

shown in Figure 7.26, which consists of two flat boards which are slapped shut by means of handles. It is probable that the slapstick reached its hey-day during the vaudeville era when the pit drummer was called upon to accompany the stage comic's pantomime with sound effects.

SLEIGH BELLS

Sleigh bells used as musical instruments are highly suggestive of Christmas, Santa Claus, sleigh rides, etc. Waldteufel, Leroy Anderson, and even Mahler (*Fourth Symphony*) have scored for sleigh bells. The most convenient way to play rhythm figures cleanly on sleigh bells is to mount them on a flat board, which can then be shaken up and down. See Figure 7.27. To play softly, damp several of the bells with the hand and allow only two or three to vibrate.

Figure 7.27. Sleigh bells.

CHAPTER 8

Latin-American Instruments

In this chapter descriptions, photos of correct playing positions, techniques, and idiomatic rhythm figures of the percussion instruments generally classified as Latin-American rhythm instruments are given. In dance bands the rhythm patterns as given can be used. Concert band and orchestra arrangements usually have parts for these instruments written out, although often it is desirable to substitute authentic beats for those notated. The Latin instruments are easily obtainable and are relatively inexpensive. All school bands and orchestras should have claves, maracas, guiro, bongos, and cowbell at the disposal of their percussion sections.

CLAVES

The claves are rosewood sticks about 6″ or 7″ long and about an inch in diameter. In a good matched pair one clave will be of a higher pitch than its mate. The claves are very important in the dance rhythms of Afro-Cuban origin, namely the rhumba, bolero, beguine, mambo, cha-cha-cha, and guaracha.

In these dances they play a two measure pattern: which is repeated over and over from start to finish of the piece. The pattern measures may be reversed if the rhythmic structure of the melody conforms more closely to that order: In either case the pattern, once set, is never changed.

One clave rests lightly between the ends of the fingers and thumb of the left hand with the palm up and cupped to add resonance. This stationary clave is struck by the right clave held lightly in a natural grasp. The less contact of flesh with the claves, the more resonant the tone. See Figure 8.1.

Two round pieces of hardwood approximately 6″ long and 1″ in diameter can be procured very easily from any school woodshop, and can serve as an inexpensive substitute for the authentic claves.

Figure 8.1. Claves.

MARACAS

The maracas are hollow gourds, or plastic substitutes, filled with shot or seeds and fitted with handles. They are used in all Latin dances except the tango.

The most important basic function of the maracas is to provide a steady flow to the music by sounding a continuous eighth note pattern:

It is usually best to stick strictly to this eighth note rhythm, although authentic Latin players often add to or modify this beat.

Figure 8.2. Maracas.

Shake the maracas up and down in short arcs, using a sharp wrist motion in order to cause the seeds to strike the inside of the shells simultaneously. This will help to make the sound crisp and rhythmic. To produce a good sound for soft passages and to avoid the grace note effect, hold the maracas as shown and tap on the top of them with the forefinger of each hand.

The samba is an exception to the foregoing in that both maracas are held in the right hand, one up and one down. The rocking motion of the right forearm, back and then forward, is done either in a quarter note rhythm with the second and fourth quarter accented: , or in eighths, with every second eighth accented:

Figure 8.3. Method of holding maracas for the samba.

COWBELL

The cowbell is a necessary ingredient of the modern Cuban rhythm section in playing the mambo, cha-cha-cha, and also in the Brazilian samba. The cowbell is held in the left hand with the large end to the right.

Figure 8.4. Cowbell.

It is usually struck with a snare drumstick, but it can also be struck with a clave which has been well wrapped with tape. A variety of tones can be obtained from the cowbell, depending upon which part of the bell is struck. Cowbells less than 6″ long do not produce a full enough tone for an authentic sound. The cowbell as it comes from the music store is not ready for use until it has been wrapped near its large end with several winds of tape. An unwrapped cowbell usually emits too harsh a clang, and the tape serves to deaden it somewhat.

A simple basic beat for the mambo is:

where the first and third beats of the measure are loud (open end of the bell) and the second and fourth beats are softer because they are played near the closed end. See diagram page 136. Typical variants for the mambo and cha-cha-cha are:

Cha-cha-cha

The pattern for the samba is:

The dome of a cymbal struck with the shoulder of a snare drumstick may serve as a substitute for the cowbell.

BONGOS

Figure 8.5. Bongos.

The bongo player is the "free agent" of the Latin percussion section, since he is not expected to stick rigidly to a steady rhythm pattern but is free to improvise "fill-ins" and "licks" as the spirit moves. The bongos themselves are small bucket-like single-headed drums which are held between the seated player's knees, with the deeper toned bongo to the right. The bongos should be tuned so that their interval corresponds to a third or fourth.

Bongos are struck with the extended index and middle fingers of both the right and left hands. In symphonic scores it may be necessary to use small snare drumsticks or timbale dowels to obtain sufficient volume. The piercing "pop" of the bongo is achieved by the simultaneous striking of the edge (rim) and the head proper, as in the snare drum rimshot. Since this is done with the fingers, however, it is rather painful until the player has toughened up his fingers through much bongo playing. The novice or school player will probably find that one or more of the beats given following will suffice for the bulk of his playing. He should not, at the beginning, try for fancy "licks."

Basic beats for

Rhumba

R L R L R   L R L   R R low

Bolero and Beguine

R R L R L R L   R R

Mambo

R   R L R L   R R

Fast Mambo

R   R L R L   R

Cha-cha-cha

R R R L   R R R   L

CONGA DRUM

The conga drum is the large single-headed drum which is slung over the shoulder, held between the knees, or fitted with adjustable legs. Other names for this instrument are *tumbadora*, or simply *tumba*. In appearance it resembles an elongated nail keg, and its main function is to provide a steady bass-register beat.

Figure 8.6. Conga drum.

The basic pattern following may be played in the rhumba, mambo, bolero, beguine, cha-cha-cha. It is not generally used in the samba or tango. The basic beat for the conga is:

The extended fingers of the left hand strike the drumhead lightly on the first and third counts of the measure, while the right hand plays the second beat at the edge with fingers extended and the "four-and" with the flat of the hand in the center of the drumhead. The edge tone is rather high in pitch, while the tone at the center is very deep. Pitch gradations can be obtained by placing the elbow of the left arm on the head and exerting different pressure while playing with the R hand.

A tom-tom or snare drum with snares off may substitute for the conga drum. Because the rims of the tom-tom or snare drum make the hand and finger technique painful for the player's right hand, a drumstick or mallet can be used to sound the second and fourth beats.

GUIRO

The guiro is made from the shell of a dried gourd, or may be made of wood in the shape of a fat cigar. Its top surface is notched, and holes are cut in the under side for the thumb and fingers of the left hand, used to hold the instrument. When a stick, back of a comb, triangle beater, or two-pronged wire scraper is rubbed across the notched surface, a resonant scratch-

Figure 8.7. Guiro.

ing sound is emitted. Other names for the guiro are gourd, scratcher, scraper, reco-reco.

Various rhythms are used in the several Latin dance forms. Some of the typical patterns are:

1. Slow rhumba, bolero

2. Fast rhumba, mambo

3. Cha-cha-cha

4. Samba

TIMBALES

The pair of timbales are used in authentic Latin bands as the basic drum sound. The distinctive feature of the timbales is their metal shell, usually of copper or spun brass. Timbales have only top heads, which are tucked directly on the counterhoops—there are no flesh hoops. The pair of drums are mounted on a stand with the higher pitched drum to the right. The usual dimensions for timbales are 7″ x 13″ and 7″ x 14″. Very often a cowbell is mounted between the timbales. The table of percussion instruments in Chapter 2 contains an illustration of the timbales.

Timbales are played with either very small drumsticks or dowels about 3/8″ in diameter, held in the overhand manner of the timpani stick. Rolls are single stroked. Rim shots are frequently utilized for the fill-in beats which lend color and excitement to the mambo, cha-cha-cha, etc. In the slow Latin dances such as the bolero and beguine, the "paila" style is employed. "Paila" means literally *pail,* and to play in this style the right stick strikes against the outer shell of the high timbale in a steady eighth note pattern, while the left stick alternates the afterbeats on the heads of the two drums. Some of the typical timbale beats are:

Paila

Mambo

Cha-cha-cha

in which the left stick is held across the snare drum so that its butt end is on the head, and the shoulder of the stick makes contact with the rim, indicated in the foregoing by the x's. Figure 8.8 shows the snare drum being played in this manner.

Figure 8.8. Stick positions for Latin-American beats on the snare drum.

The beats for the several Latin rhythm instruments contained in the preceding section may be substituted for written-out parts as scored in band and orchestra arrangements of Latin music. In most cases the arrangers of these selections have been content to notate parts for the rhythm instruments without a working knowledge of the authentic beats used by the Latin players themselves.

The bass drum is not considered to be a Latin rhythm instrument, but it is often helpful to use it to help maintain good rhythm in the band or orchestra. When the bass drum is used it should *always* play one of the following patterns:

1. For Bolero, Beguine, Mambo, Cha-cha-cha

2. For Samba

3. For Tango

The bass drum should *never* anticipate the third beat of the measure thus:

. This is an obsolete rhumba beat once used by American drummers. It has never been used by authentic Latin players, although many arrangements still appear with this incorrect bass beat.

The snare drum with snares turned off may be substituted for the timbales, and American drummers have developed a cross-stick technique for Latin playing. A good basic beat for the mambo and cha-cha-cha is:

The pattern for the snare drum in the slower dances, such as the bolero, is:

As an aid in adapting the Latin-American rhythm instruments for use by the full percussion section of the band or orchestra, the following composite pattern measures are given following.

Bolero, beguine

Mambo

CHAPTER 9

Set Drumming

Dance band, stage band, and jazz drumming are highly specialized skills, and it is difficult to present adequate concepts via the printed page. The eager and interested student may be guided using the information and suggestions contained in this chapter, but for that student who shows real aptitude for this phase of percussion playing, it is strongly recommended that private study, listening, watching, and trying out for himself the techniques of the modern jazz drummer follow up the introductory stages. Every well-rounded percussionist must have a basic knowledge of the fundamental dance rhythms and should have an opportunity to practice with a pedal bass drum set-up. The author would strongly recommend that every student percussionist, at some point early in his school career, be given some training and guidance in the technique and style of dance band drumming. Music instructors from elementary school through college would reap many benefits from encouraging, rather than discouraging, their drum students to play jazz. Not only are dance band and jazz drumming fun and hence interest-building devices, but the rhythmic discipline and precision required in these styles of music contribute to the total musical development of the student. For those students who develop their talents sufficiently, there is the additional prospect of earning money to help defray college tuition expenses and a later vocational or avocational source of income.

The usual dance band set consists of a bass drum with pedal, snare drum, one or two top cymbals, sock (variously called hi-hat, foot, off-beat, after-beat, etc.) cymbals with foot pedal stand, one small mounted tom-tom and one large floor tom-tom, plus a cowbell. As a basic minimum for any kind of dance band, the drummer must have a bass drum with pedal and a

Courtesy Ludwig Drum Co.

Figure 9.1. Dance band drum set.

snare drum with floor stand. The best size bass drum is a 22″ diameter model, and for the snare drum the 5 1/2″ or 6″ models are the most popular. Starting with these absolutely essential items, next would be added a top cymbal on shell-mounted holder or floor stand, preferably an 18″ to 20″ diameter. Next in importance is the sock cymbal set-up, using 13″, 14″, or 15″ cymbals. For additional information on the make, type, and diameters of cymbals for dance band use, refer back to the Chapter 4 section on Cymbals. One small 9″ x 13″ tom-tom, shell mounted, is the next logical addition. For Latin music, a large cowbell is indispensible (it should be wound with tape to eliminate the excess ring). A large 16″ x 16″ tom-tom with legs attached would round out the set to that normally carried by the professional drummer.

There are three basic functions of the dance band drummer. The one which is most often overlooked completely by the novice is in fact the most important, namely the providing of a steady beat upon which the group can lean. In addition to keeping a steady beat, he must contribute interesting and musical fill-ins and "licks." His third function would be to take an occasional break of 2, 4, or 8 measures, and very occasionally he might solo for a whole chorus or more. The instructor and students should discuss fully the implications of the foregoing statements. Many young students are completely unaware of the qualifications necessary for good dance and jazz drumming and of the real contribution of the drummer to the total ensemble.

BASIC 4/4 PATTERNS FOR FOXTROT AND JAZZ

One important rhythm pattern that is necessary for dance or jazz playing must be learned so thoroughly that it becomes an automatic response. The beat is usually written:

but is often played with a more relaxed, or jazz, feel, approximating the notation

The beat should be practiced using the R stick only (it is nearly always played with one brush or one stick) on the pad. Various tempos should be set and maintained over a number of repetitions of the one measure figure. When this can be done fairly automatically, add the R foot, tapping on all 4 beats of the measure:

This is called "4-beat."

Next, try beating the R foot only on 1 and 3, keeping the same R stick pattern.

This is called "2-beat."

The L stick's job is to furnish the strong after-beat characteristic of much dance (foxtrot) and jazz music. We now have:

and in "2-beat":

Note that the R and L sticks coincide exactly on beats 2 and 4.

The final coordination to be added is the L foot, which operates the sock cymbal pedal. Like the L stick, its function is to emphasize the after-beat. The sock cymbal maintains its afterbeat pattern with rigid monotony, regardless of any L stick variations and in total disregard of the bass drum's pattern.

In "4-beat":

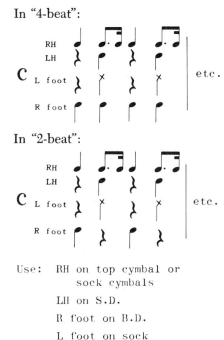

In "2-beat":

Use: RH on top cymbal or
          sock cymbals
       LH on S.D.
       R foot on B.D.
       L foot on sock
          cymbal pedal

This completes the basic foxtrot (jazz) drum pattern. The student should practice the pattern as given at the drum set until it is quite automatic, a task requiring considerable perseverance. *Only* when this elemental pattern has been made secure can the player's thought be extended to the embellishing figures which serve to create interest through variation. Again, the author would strongly urge *analytical listening* to experienced and talented modern drummers on record, TV, radio, and especially in live performance. The student should have no qualms about copying the styles and tricks of his favorite players. The materials of the modern dance drummer are a composite heritage of styles and tricks passed along from drummer to drummer over the past sixty-odd years, and are in truth "public domain."

Figure 9.2. R stick on ride cymbal, L on snare drum. Over-shoulder view.

Figure 9.3. Same as Figure 9.2. Side view.

Figure 9.4. Playing rhythm with brushes. Over-shoulder view.

Figure 9.5. Same as 9.4. Side view.

FILL-INS AND SOLOS

The modern drummer has an opportunity to assert his creativity in improvising fill-ins, two and four measure breaks, and extended solos. Since the advent of so-called progressive jazz in the late 1940's, the style of drumming has undergone a radical change from the older conception which emphasized a steady, swinging beat underlined principally by a rigid and heavy bass drum. Today's drummer keeps the "time" mainly by the ride cymbal rhythm and thus frees the bass drum foot from its former monotonous duty. This new freedom makes possible left hand and right foot combinations which serve both to punctuate the flow of the music and to fill in gaps in the melodic structure behind ensemble riffs and during improvised solos by the other instruments. Such fill-ins vary in length from a single well-placed note to a measure or more. No rule can be laid down regarding the placement of tasteful fills, except to state that they can often be inserted at the ends of phrases. The fill-in should have the quality of *leading in* to the next musical idea or providing a rhythmic springboard from which the ensemble or soloist can surge forward. For this reason most fills should arrive at their climax with a heavy accent on the first beat of the new phrase. Three rather simple examples of fill-ins are notated following.

Short solos of two, four, or eight bars duration are sometimes called breaks. The novice is well advised to work out and memorize some two-measure patterns before attempting longer solo breaks. He must keep in mind that whatever he plays must be interesting and, more importantly, maintain the pulse of the beat. It therefore is best to keep the pattern simple enough so that the rhythm will be perfectly clear to himself, the other musicians, and the listeners. When working out such two-bar breaks in practice sessions it is a good policy to count each beat aloud or mentally. Three examples of simple two measure breaks follow.

When the student has perfected several two-bar break patterns, various combinations of these can be strung together to form four measure phrases. It is important to keep the count, either orally or mentally, during practice. By this means a feeling for the phrase can be acquired. Eventually the drummer will wish to improvise four bar breaks without dependence upon previously worked-out patterns, and should in time develop a sense of phrasing which will permit him to fill in the four bars without counting each beat. The same remarks would apply generally to the eight measure solo break. Longer solos, however, require more musical planning, that is, the drummer should structure his solo so that it will show not only his

EXAMPLES OF SIMPLE TWO MEASURE BREAKS

technique but also his musical feeling. This is not easy for everyone to accomplish, and requires long hours of practice at the drum set. Several suggestions may help to guide the novice:

1. Try to have an idea for a rhythmic motif *before* launching into the solo.
2. Begin softly and with a fairly simple exposition of the motif.
3. Stay with either a duple or triple division of the beats and build toward a climax, then introduce a new idea.
4. Save the heavy cymbal crashes for the final climax.
5. Don't try to fill up every beat with 32nd notes! A few well-placed rests during the solo can be very effective.
6. Try to get contrasts in volume, motion, and timbre.
7. Spend a lot of time listening analytically to live or recorded drum solos.
8. Practice working out ideas at the drum set.

READING STOCK AND SPECIAL ARRANGEMENTS

Arrangers of popular, commercial, and jazz music do not attempt to write their drum parts literally. Instead, they notate the skeletal outline and trust that the player will have the requisite skill and experience in the various styles to interpret and embellish the part. This is a good system, for it minimizes reading difficulties (which would be great indeed if arrangers wrote out everything exactly as they wished it to be played), and it allows an outlet for the creativeness of the individual drummer. An example often cited by writers on jazz notation to illustrate the comparative freedom of interpretation in this idiom is the standard cymbal ride rhythm:

May be played as follows:

It is assumed by the arranger that the drummer will choose from among these various possible interpretations the one which "feels right" for the tempo and style of the arrangement. In other words, the ride rhythm figure ♩ ♪♩ ♫ is a notational convenience or conventionalized way of indicating any or all of the foregoing examples. And so it is with many of the conventionalized notational usages in drum parts, or "charts," to borrow from the jazzman's jargon. For example, the chart may indicate only the rhythm figures that are to be played *with the ensemble*, leaving long sections marked simply "16 bars straight rhythm," "light rhythm next 8," "32 bars shuffle," etc. It is expected that the drummer will know what is meant by these conventionalized signals and govern his interpretation accordingly. Stock arrangements usually have every measure written out, but the drummer does not take them literally. In both stock drum parts and special arrangement charts the drummer should observe carefully the introductions, first and second endings, indicated fill-ins and solo spots, and endings in order to play the tutti licks in unison with the ensemble. The remainder of the phrases will usually be played with an appropriate steady rhythm figure, and whether or not the measures are written out or simply indicated, they should be counted in order to keep the place. In most situations the drum part should be considered as a guide, rather than played literally, in the sense that the percussion part of a symphonic composition would be played "as written."

SOCK CYMBAL TECHNIQUE

Many drummers use a rocking motion of the left toe and heel in playing afterbeats on the sock (hi-hat) cymbals. The heel is lifted off the pedal as the toe is depressed on the second and fourth beats of the 4/4 measure. This style of playing the sock cymbals is less fatiguing to the ankle and leg muscles than the constant straight downward press of the toe section of the foot. Another advantage is that the rocking motion helps to maintain a steady beat.

In playing the ride rhythm figure ♩ ♪♩ ♫ with the stick on the sock cymbals, the foot continues its strict afterbeat pattern. This will produce an open sound on the first and third beats, closed sounds on the second and fourth. Most drummers prefer to cross the R over the left to reach the sock cymbals, as illustrated in Figure 9.6. For loud playing the cymbals are opened an inch or more. The amount of opening is controlled by the left foot; for wide opening use large rocking motions, for less open-

Figure 9.6. R stick on sock cymbal.

ing use smaller motions. A good effect can be obtained by allowing the cymbals to separate only slightly when playing the ride rhythm. In this way the cymbals continue to "zizz" against each other during the first and third beats. This style is particularly effective behind legato ensemble writing, and can be used as a contrast to the more choppy open-and-closed style.

The R stick may either strike the cymbals at an angle (shoulder of stick) or, for a softer effect, the tip of the stick may be used on the top of the upper cymbal.

Remember that whether or not the sticks are playing rhythm on the sock cymbals, the basic afterbeat produced by the rocking motion of the left foot is continued.

SPECIAL STUDY FOR SPEED

THREE HAND AND FOOT COORDINATION STUDIES

BASIC DRUM PATTERNS FOR VARIOUS DANCES

The dance band drummer must be conversant with other common dance rhythms in addition to the foxtrot pattern. There follow typical basic drum patterns of some of the more common dances. Many of these dances are dated and are seldom played by today's bands; however, they are still called for, occasionally, and a passing knowledge of them will assist the drummer. Like the foxtrot pattern, these are skeletal and would need embellishment and variation to sound authentic.

BASIC WALTZ BEAT

The waltz is the easiest of the common dance beats. It should be played rather "straight" and be fairly free from "fill-ins."

Use: Brushes, usually. Loud last choruses will require sticks in a large band. If desired, the drummer may swish the L brush during the 2nd and 3rd beats and the two written ♩'s with the R brush. This is for "American" or rather slow waltzes. The faster Viennese waltz requires sticks, and is played with the characteristic anticipation of the 2nd beat:

TANGO

The tango is also a fairly regular beat. It should be played with a good drive and heavy accents on the final eighth of each measure. Do not turn off the snares.

BOLERO

The rhumba as such has been ousted from its place as the foremost Latin American dance by the bolero, mambo, and cha-cha-cha. The dance which corresponds most closely to the slow rhumba is called the bolero, and its basic beat is:

Snares off. Use of sock cym. is optional. There are a number of variations possible in the bolero, especially in the timbres used. The Latin drummer plays a steady eighth note pattern on the metal shell of his R timbale, playing a pattern of

with his L hand on the pair of timbales. Most American drummers use the L stick held across the snare drum so that its butt end is on the head, and the shoulder of the stick makes contact with the rim. This might be notated thus:

x above the note means L stick on rim. The bass drum pattern should be observed carefully.

Figure 9.7 shows the drummer playing a bolero.

MAMBO

The second rhumba derivative is the mambo, which means literally "Cuban Jazz." Like American jazz it has a monotonous driving beat upon which various ensemble riffs and solos are grounded. There is a definite tendency for our American jazz to incorporate some of the elements of the Latin style, and conversely, their music is constantly under the influence of our modern jazz. The basic mambo ingredients are a heavy cowbell on the first and third beats, and a continuous pattern played on timbales, conga drums, or on snare drum and tom-tom. The bass drum has several options, but it is not under any obligation to play a unison rhythm pattern with the string bass, as it is usually required to do in other dance music. One basic mambo pattern might be notated thus:

The authenticity of this basic pattern will be enhanced if the player uses the tip of the R stick near the clamp end of the cowbell on the ♪♪'s, and plays the heavily accented ♩'s with the shoulder of the stick at the open end of the bell. This is diagrammed following.

The L hand notes should be split between two pitches, a high (snare drum with snares off) on the 2nd beat and a lower sound (small tom-tom) on the 4th beat. As a variation useful in final loud ensemble choruses

or behind trumpet or piano montunas (long, free solos based on one or two chords), the cowbell beat

may be transferred to the top cymbal. A good effect is to strike the cymbal on the dome section, alternating the tips and shoulders of the R stick. An example of the kind of variation often used by Latin drummers for the R hand on the cymbal dome:

CHA-CHA-CHA

Figure 9.8. Drummer playing a cha-cha-cha.

The cha-cha-cha drum pattern is basically very similar to the mambo. The tempo for most cha-chachas is fairly slow, however, which allows time for the quick cowbell grace notes shown in the example below. Figure 9.8 illustrates the position of the drummer as he plays the fourth beat in the cha-cha-cha measure.

SAMBA

This dance was imported from Brazil, and is basically in "2 beat" rhythm. The bass drum plays strictly on 1 and 3 of a ¢ measure, as in a march or polka: [notation] . The L is played with a brush, and provides the afterbeats [notation] . The ♩ on the 2nd beat should be pushed down into the head, while the ♫'s on the 4th beat should be "open." The R has a tricky pattern, played with a stick on cowbell or snare drumhead:

[notation]

The combined pattern is:

[notation]

If two cowbells are available, a good effect is gained by alternating the high bell on the first pair of [notation] 's and the low bell on the next [notation]. The sock cymbal can be used on the 2 and 4.

BOSSA NOVA

The bossa nova is based on the foregoing samba and is also in a "2 beat" rhythm. The bass drum plays the following pattern:

[notation]

The left foot plays the sock cymbal on the 2 and 4 beats—

[notation]

The right hand plays a pattern of straight eight notes on the cymbal with a snare stick or brush

The left hand plays with a snare stick which has been placed on the snare drum so that its butt end is on the head and the shoulder of the stick makes contact with the rim. The left hand then lifts only the end of the stick touching the rim for accented beats

[notation]

The combined pattern is:

[notation]

ROCK BEAT

Starting in the early 1960's, the "rock and roll" music took its place in the forefront of the pop music field. A definite "rock" style developed culminating in its use in musicals and even a "rock opera." As is the case with any beat style, there are many possible and acceptable variations; however, the rock beat has as its basic ingredients the following:

[notation]

The right hand can easily be converted to triplets to give a ternary feeling:

[notation]

CHAPTER 10

The Marching Band Percussion Section

INSTRUMENTATION

The percussion instruments used in the marching band are one or more field drums, tenor drum(s), cymbals, bass drum(s), and bell-lyra. Bands of forty or less pieces should have two snare drummers, one cymbal player and one bass drummer. Bands of from forty to seventy-five should have three snare drummers, cymbal player, and bass drummer, with bell-lyra optional. Hundred, or hundred-plus, piece bands often use up to six snare drummers, two tenor drummers, one or two cymbal players, one or two bass drummers, and one or two bell-lyra players.

The marching band percussionist must add showmanship to musicianship to be effective in these days of spectacle-type marching band entertainments. Snare drummers should play with open rudiments, plenty of full arm strokes, and all the snare drummers must use identical stickwork and equal stick arcs. If tenor

Courtesy Ludwig Drum Co.

Figure 10.1. Northwestern University Marching Band Percussion Section.

Figure 10.2. Tenor drumstick handhold, step 1.

Figure 10.3. Tenor drumstick handhold, step 2.

Figure 10.4. Twirling the tenor drumstick.

drums are used, the players must practice synchronizing their twirling sticks as well as their actual notes. The Scotch style of bass drumming is usually employed in the marching band. This technique makes use of two beaters with looped thongs which lace around the players' fingers and wrist so as to allow for twirling. Both heads of the bass drum are played upon. Cymbal players should use plenty of motion in the ordinary up-and-down strokes, and extend the cymbals well over head in the flare stroke used for solo crashes.

The table following can be used as a guide for the purchase of marching band percussion equipment. For flashy appearance and durability the so-called pearl, or sparkling pearl, finishes are recommended. Their slightly higher cost is well justified. Plastic heads on all drums to be used out of door are recommended.

THE TENOR DRUM

The tenor drum can be played slung over the shoulder in the manner of the snare drum, or it can be carried by means of the vertical holder in front of the player's chest and played with the Scotch bass drum technique. The latter method offers more possibilities for flash and is easier on the player than the traditional sling. Manufacturers' catalogs contain photos and information about the vertical tenor drum holder. Tenor drumsticks are equipped with hard felt beater balls and thongs which interlace through the player's fingers to make twirling of the sticks possible. Most tenor drum parts consist mainly of single notes. Should a roll be called for, the single stroke timpani-style roll is used.

Recommended Equipment Specifications,
Marching Band Percussion Instruments

School level	snare	tenor	bass	cymbals
Junior High	double tension 10″ x 14″		double tension 10″ x 26″	15″ medium
High	double tension 12″ x 15″	double tension 12″ x 17″	double tension 10″ x 28″	16″ medium
College, University, and Adult	double tension 12″ x 16″	double tension 12″ x 17″	double tension 10″ x 28″	18″ medium

The tone of the tenor drum should be midway in general pitch range between that of the snare drum and bass drum. Its heads will not ordinarily need to be tensioned as much as those of the snare drum. A very suitable substitute for the tenor drum is a field drum with its snares removed or simply turned off.

TUNING THE PERCUSSION SECTION

Much neglected is the "tuning" of the percussion section of a marching band. It is a time consuming task and one which must be supervised (at least in the public schools) by the director. In the more mature organizations, the section leader usually can handle this. The results are well worth the efforts.

First of all, it should be pointed out that the extent to which this "tuning" is carried is entirely contingent upon the desires of the individual director. As an absolute minimum, all like instruments should be "tuned" or tensioned to the same response, i.e., all snare drums should sound alike, etc.

As the next logical step, there should be a low, medium, and high response range from the section as a whole utilizing the bass, tenors, and snares, respectively. Otherwise, much of the effectiveness of modern day "antiphonal" percussion cadences is lost.

To carry this tuning process to its ultimate, a triad can be created using the bass as the tonic, the tenors as the third, and the snares as the fifth of the triad. This gives depth of sound not only to the percussion section, but also to the entire band. It assists in projection and "cleanness" of sound of the percussion section and gives a true meaning to the term "antiphonal cadence."

GENERAL INFORMATION

The best placement in the block marching formation for the percussion is a center rank, or ranks.

A useful device for maneuvering the band without creating excessive sound is for the snare drummers to tap out a cadence, using the shoulders of the sticks on the rims of the snare drums.

Web slings for carrying field snare drums and tenor drums are included in the purchase price of new instruments, as are one pair of sticks or beaters. The sling passes over the right shoulder, from right to left across the front and back of the chest, and suspends the drum on the player's left side about belt high. To put on the sling preparatory to attaching the drum: 1-grasp the latch (heavier) end with the right hand, eyelet at the top; 2-grasp hook (lighter) end with the left hand; 3-stretch left arm out away from body;

TRADITIONAL MARCHING BEATS

1. Funeral March Beat —— muffle S.D.

S.D.

B.D. & cym.

2. Old French Street Beat

3. The Roll-off

The Roll-off

4-bring right hand up over head and then down across front of chest so that sling rests on right shoulder, and 5-put hook through eyelet. When ready to play, bring the drum up to playing level with the left hand, and latch through carrying hook on the rim of the drum. See Chapter 3, page 35 and 36, Figures 3.26 to 3.29.

A device called a *leg rest* is now on the market which attaches to the lower portion of the field drum or tenor drum and has a crescent-shaped metal strip which fits around the player's leg above the knee. The leg rest is adjustable and holds the drum in playing position at all times, thus eliminating bruised legs and missed beats caused by the drum's twisting in windy weather. Also available is the device known as a "hi-stepper" mentioned in Chapter 3. This device positions the drum up, out, and away from the body and legs. This gives more freedom of movement to the drummer and maximum control of the drum. Its use almost necessitates playing with the matched grip.

Stick beats are called for in some marches and are frequently utilized in marching cadences. The stick beat is made by clicking the snare drumsticks together in mid-air. The usual method is to strike the shoulder of the L stick with the shoulder of the R stick at a point about chest high over the drum. Notes to be played as stick beats are marked with X's above the noteheads. A few of the traditional rudimental drum solos make use of stick beats.

The percussion section of a marching band must perform musically to be effective. This means the section must play dynamics, *not just loudly*. It must read music, although it should have well-rehearsed fake patterns for all common meters which it can utilize from time to time. The section should not be used continually. Besides the fact that percussionists need to rest periodically, the relief offered by the complete absence of the percussion sound is often extremely effective.

CADENCES

Drum beats used on the march are called cadences, street beats, or tap steps. The following cadences are scored for field drums, cymbals, and bass drum, with a few containing parts for the tenor drums as well.

6.

TWO TYPICAL MODERN STREET BEATS

7.

8.

Add flams on accented beats in #7 and #8 for a more martial sound.

CADENCES WITH TENOR DRUM ADDED

Cadences 9 through 13 utilize the contemporary concept of interplay between the various percussion "voices," particularly between the snare drum and tenor drum parts. The cadences get progressively more difficult.

9.

S. D.

Ten. D.

Cym.
B. D.

S. D.

Ten. D.

Cym.
B. D.

Appendix

SELECTION, CARE AND STORAGE OF PERCUSSION EQUIPMENT

Determining basic needs. Persons charged with the responsibility of purchasing and maintaining percussion instruments must be aware of the minimum essential needs of their particular musical organization. In many school districts it is customary for all instruments to be issued from a central office, while in others the instrumental music teacher makes purchases direct from local retail houses from either district or school funds. Under either plan, it behooves the persons responsible to make the best possible use of the monies available. The *Guide* has included recommended specifications for all of the instruments in several of the chapters by means of tables classified by school grade level. As a further aid in determining the percussion instruments which should make up the basic inventory for the various school groups, the following are suggested lists.

Elementary School
(orchestra and/or band)

bass drum

pair of cymbals

concert snare drum (one or more)

triangle

tambourine

woodblock

set of bells

castanets

sticks, stands, beaters, holders as needed for foregoing items

Junior High School
(orchestra and/or band)

pair of timpani

bass drum

concert snare drum (one or more)

pair of cymbals

suspended cymbal

set of bells

triangle

tambourine

woodblock

castanets

Latin rhythm instruments

sticks, stands, beater, holders as needed for foregoing items

if band marches, add Scotch bass drum, one or more field drums

High School
(orchestra and/or band)

3 or 4 timpani

bass drum

concert snare drum (one or more)

field drum (one or more)

pair of cymbals

suspended cymbal

set of bells

xylophone

chimes

tam-tam (gong)

triangle (small and large)

tambourine

woodblock

temple blocks

castanets

Latin rhythm instruments

sticks, beaters, stands and holders as needed for fore-going items

for marching band, add

Scotch bass drum, smaller pair of cymbals, one or two tenor drums, bell-lyra

for dance band set-up, see Chapter 9 page 129.

College, University or Professional Orchestra or Concert band

set of four timpani

bass drum

concert snare drum (one or more)

field drum (one or more)

set of concert tom-toms (4)

pairs of cymbals (two sizes)

two suspended cymbals (two sizes)

set of bells

xylophone

vibraphone

marimba

chimes

tam-tam (gong)

triangles (3)

woodblocks (2)

tambourines (2)

temple blocks

castanets

sleigh bells

ratchet

Latin rhythm instruments

sticks, beaters, stands and holders as needed for fore-going items

for marching band, add Scotch bass drum(s), additional pair of cymbals, one or two tenor drums, one or two bell-lyras

for dance band set-up, see Chapter 9, page 129.

Care of percussion equipment. Much unnecessary wear and tear on percussion equipment results from ignorance of proper procedures for routine care or from failure to heed common sense rules of instrument care.

Drumheads are easily damaged and broken and account for a large part of the percussion repair bills, yet it is quite possible to make heads wear and retain their life if they are given good care. Snare drum batter (top) heads should be set at an even and tight playing tension (with equal tension on each tuning rod) on a dry day when the head is contracted to its maximum. The snare (bottom) head should be set at this time also, but not quite so tightly as the batter head. A tight batter head depresses *only slightly* when at proper playing tension; the snare head depresses a little more. One very important point: *do not* change the tension once it has been satisfactorily set. Constant loosening and tightening soon causes the head to slip on the flesh hoop, and eventually it is impossible to keep it taut. The only time one would need to use the tuning key would be when required to play the drum on a very rainy, humid day, when the head would be too slack to play on. If it is tightened up under such circumstances be sure to loosen it the same amount after playing, as if there is a

quick drop in the humidity a split head can result. There is one additional reason for tightening the heads, and that is the natural settling and stretching of the calfskin. A newly mounted head, for instance, will require several tensionings before it is settled. For long periods of storage, loosen calfskin drumheads about 1/2 turn. Plastic heads need not be loosened for storage. Additional information about drumhead care, with particular reference to plastic heads, is contained in Chapter 3, pages 25-27.

The wire brushes, if used a good deal in dance band playing, will tend to blacken and roughen up a calfskin batter head. One good way to prevent this roughing up (the wires eventually poke tiny holes in the head) is to bend the last 3/8″ of the wires upward with a pair of pliers. This will prevent them from digging into the head, as they then strike or rotate at an angle. This procedure is not necessary if a plastic batter head is used.

Instructors, conductors and percussionists will find it most convenient, practical and economical in the long run to purchase drumheads ready mounted on the flesh hoops. Be sure, when ordering by mail or by phone, to give the exact diameter of the shell as measured from *outside to outside* edges. When mounting plastic heads, make sure that the portion of the drum's shell over which the head passes is absolutely smooth. See Chapter 3, pages 26-27 for the step-by-step procedure used to mount drumheads.

Bass drumheads should be cared for in quite a different manner from the snare drumheads. Most bass drumhead trouble stems from a failure to tune with an equal number of half-turns at each tuning handle. On all drumheads, equal tension at all points around the circumference is absolutely requisite to good tone production. The collar should be measured with a ruler when setting the tension on a newly mounted bass drumhead. The hoop (rim) should protrude an equal amount from the head at each tuning handle.

Another important matter which is often overlooked is the proper tuning of the bass drumheads. Unlike the snare drum, they should be changed before and after each use. For detailed instructions concerning the tuning of the bass drum for playing and storage, see Chapter 4, page 64. Plastic bass drumheads do not require these routine adjustments.

Timpani heads should be cared for in much the same manner as the calfskin bass drumheads. Equality of tension around the circumference is of the utmost importance. After the playing period on a day when the humidity is average, set the 25″ kettle to *d* and the 28″ kettle to *A*. This will put about the right degree of tension on the heads for storage. Timpani heads should *not* be loosened to their lowest notes for storage. It is much better for the life of the head to keep it under tension. On very humid days leave the heads a tone or so lower than the usual *d* and *A* to allow for a possible sudden weather change.

See the section on *Timpani Heads*, Chapter 6, pages 96-97, for additional information, particularly regarding plastic heads. The procedure for "wetting down" timpani heads as a means of prolonging their life is also contained in that section.

To eliminate the annoying squeaks and creaks often emitted by the timpani when the heads are being stretched in tuning, rub lanolin, paraffin or powdered graphite around the entire perimeter of the bowl on its top edge where it comes in direct contact with the head. (The head must be removed from the bowl for this operation.)

To prevent the spread of a small tear in a timpani head (calfskin type) cauterize by heating the point of a needle red hot and pierce the head to form a tiny circular hole at each end of the tear. Breaks in the head up to a couple of inches in length can be rendered harmless by this method. The head should not then be played upon at the point of the tear.

Adhesive or Scotch tape should not be used in an attempt to repair a kettledrum head, as even a small piece of tape deadens the tone considerably. Tears, holes, or breaks too large to cauterize will necessitate replacement of the head. Save the discarded timpani head—portions of it can be cut out to re-head tambourines, bongos, and even snare drums.

Drums and timpani should be kept free from dust and dirt, and their chrome-plated and copper parts cleaned with the appropriate metal polish. Cymbals can be cleaned with Copper-Clean or Bon-Ami, following the directions on each can carefully. It is dangerous to buff cymbals with a power buffer, as enough heat may be generated to affect the delicate temper of the alloy.

All drumheads should be covered with fibre covers when drums are stored.

Snare tension should be left *on* when drums are not being used and for storage.

Timpani should be stored in cabinets or in fibre carrying trunks if they are not to be used for a considerable period of time or if it is necessary to leave them any place where there is danger of damage to the heads or bowls. The copper kettledrum bowls are extremely susceptible to dents. A good protective device is the hood type of padded mackintosh cover which hangs down to envelop the bowl. These can be purchased from the manufacturer or made up locally from heavy fabric, mackintosh or canvas. Moving parts of the machine timpani should be lubricated once or twice a year. Be careful not to get any oil or grease on the ratchet portion of the pedal tuning mechanism of Dresden or the old style Leedy timpani.

The moving of percussion equipment should always be supervised by the instructor of young school groups. High school and college bands and orchestras should appoint a responsible member of the percussion section to be in charge of all moving of these delicate instruments. If drayage company employees do the moving they should be well briefed on the proper handling of percussion instruments. Items which require special attention are:

1. All drum and timpani heads should be covered with fibre disk-type covers.
2. Xylophone, marimba, bell or vibraphone resonators should be wrapped or cased, as they are easily dented.
3. Timpani should be moved in their trunks. If no trunks are available, use the hoods just described. If neither trunks nor hoods are available, place timpani head down, resting on the tuning handles, and wrap the bowls with blankets.

4. Removable sets of xylophone, marimba or vibra-phone bars should be wrapped, even when moved in their cases.

5. Fibre carrying cases should be used for snare drums and for all small items such as the "traps," sticks, beaters, holders, etc.

6. Cymbals should be laid flat where nothing will rest on them. Do not toss cymbals into a box of miscellany where their edges are exposed to bending stress. A cymbal carrying bag with zipper opener is now on the market, and is highly recommended.

The life of snare drumsticks can be prolonged by making a habit of playing with the grain of the wood running at right angles to the floor. A small paint or ink mark can be used to identify the top side for easy sight checking.

Two types of percussion instrument storage cabinets are illustrated in Figures A1-A3. The cabinet shown in Figure A1 is designed for use in the band or orchestra rehearsal room. The model shown in Figures A2 and A3 doubles as a storage unit and trap table. It comes equipped with rubber casters which are not shown in the photographs.

Courtesy Norren Co.

Figure A2. Percussion storage unit.

Courtesy Norren Co.

Figure A1. Percussion storage cabinet.

Courtesy Norren Co.

Figure A3. Unit doubles as a trap table.

ASSIGNMENT OF INSTRUMENTS WITHIN THE PERCUSSION SECTION

The assignment of instruments within the percussion section of the orchestra or band may follow one or the other of two basic plans, namely, *rotation* or *specialization*. Under the policy of rotation the several percussionists would change to a different instrument for each selection or to a different instrument at each rehearsal. A policy of specialization would mean that a particular instrument would be covered at all times by a particular player. The usual specialized assignments are timpani, snare drum, cymbals, bass drum, and mallet instruments. In the large concert band the snare drum part is sometimes doubled. The small instruments such as triangle, tambourine, woodblock, and the like are usually covered by whichever percussionists are not engaged on their special instruments at the time.

In a percussion instrument class the rotation system is recommended, as every student should be given the opportunity to gain a basic playing knowledge of each of the percussion instruments. In elementary and junior high school bands and orchestras, rotation of players is also recommended, since at this stage trying out firsthand the techniques of all the instruments satisfies the tendency of young people to explore and provides a basis for later specialization. Many school instructors use a system of rotation at the beginning of each school year and continue its use until spring concert time approaches, at which time specific instrument assignments are made. These assignments are based on the particular aptitudes of the percussion section members as demonstrated throughout the earlier parts of the school year. High school situations vary, because some students enter the orchestra or band with several years of experience and/or private study on one or another of the percussion specializations, while others have only a basic generalized sort of background. Still others will likely be pianists or other instrumentalists, with little or no technical skill on any of the percussion instruments. In situations which present such diversity, the practical solution is specialization according to the training, experience, and talents of the members of the section. In high school organizations where more uniform backgrounds are to be found, rotation is probably the most satisfactory method for all concerned. The talented, ambitious, and serious student in any band or orchestra should be encouraged to develop his talents on all of the instruments. For example, a highly musical girl with several years of private study on the marimba should not only be used as the mallet specialist in the band or orchestra but also should be trained to cover some or all of the other parts. College instrumental majors who are preparing to teach music should gain as much experience as possible on all of the percussion instruments. This is often achieved by playing percussion instruments with the training orchestras or bands in addition to the major performing groups. Percussion majors should concentrate on obtaining a well-rounded skill in each of the special areas during college years. Later professional work may require their specialization in snare drum or timpani for example, but the college years are the best time to perfect techniques along the broad front in order to achieve the status of a true professional percussionist. The present-day symphony orchestra, recording, and studio professional is expected to be able to perform creditably on each and every one of the percussion instruments regardless of the particular specialized duty he may have in the orchestra.

Some policy or system should be used to insure that all the parts will be covered with a minimum of delay and discussion at rehearsals. A useful device is the penciling in of the player's first name above each entrance, instrument by instrument. In orchestrations with a separate part for each instrument the names can be written at the top of the sheet of music. In high school, college, and professional groups this method of instrument assignment works well. Assignments are usually made by the section head. In younger bands and orchestras, the instructor should make the assignments to insure equitable rotation among the students and to eliminate squabbling within the section. Parts should be marked before the music is passed out. In compositions calling for many rapid changes in instrumentation, care must be taken to consider the time factor involved in changing from one instrument to another. When one player is required to change from one instrument to another during a composition, it is helpful if a penciled notation "change to" or simply "to" is made in the music immediately after the last note played on the original instrument.

In order to illustrate the foregoing principles of making and marking part assignments, facsimiles of the percussion parts of both a band and an orchestra composition are reproduced in Figures A4 and A5.

Figure A4

Figure A4 (continued)

151

Glockenspiel, Snare Drum,
Bass Drum and Vibraphone

Figure A4 (continued)

Figure A4 (continued)

Figure A5

Figure A5 (continued)

155

HOW TO MARK PERCUSSION PARTS

In addition to the marking of instrument assignment, experience has taught percussionists the value of certain other aids to good performance which can be penciled into the parts. School music instructors should encourage their students to use pencil marks freely, following the lead of the professionals who make very liberal use of markings and rarely trust to luck or memory. There follows a list of some of the more common pencil markings used as performance aids by professional percussion players:

1. Rests, when they occur as a series of individual measures, should be numbered thus:

2. Repeat or ditto measures are very frequently encountered in drum parts. They should be numbered, either with a number for each measure, on alternate measures, or at each fourth bar, thus:

Note that the numbering corresponds with the measure *according to its place in the phrase.*

3. Cues of other instrumental parts penciled into the drum or timpani parts are often helpful as insurance against losing the count during long rests. For example:

4. Eyeglasses are conventionally used to alert the player to a trouble spot such as a quick tempo change or unexpected fermata:

5. Cuts are marked with double slash marks which include the portion of the music to be left out. These slash marks are then connected by a continuous line which may traverse bars, lines, or even pages of music. See example A below:

6. Accents and dynamic markings may be written in where they are not indicated in the score, but are desired by the conductor. Those accent and dynamic marks which require special attention may be overmarked with heavy pencil lines.

7. When abrupt changes in tempo and/or meter occur, or if there is likely to be some doubt about the conductor's choice of beat pattern, musicians usually mark the parts with slash marks above the initial measure of the piece or at the measure where a change occurs. See example B:

8. Indicate all changes of instrument or beater by "change to."

9. Timpani players should note in pencil tuning cues from other instruments during the course of a composition where frequent tunings are necessary.

10. Timpani tuning changes should be noted in pencil if they are not printed in the part, i.e., "E to F#."

11. Timpani note settings should be penciled in at the beginning of each piece or movement if they are not already printed in the part.

12. Make note of passages in mallet instrument, timpani or snare drum parts which require unusual sticking by the use of *R* and *L*.

13. Choice of most appropriate sticks, mallets or beaters should be penciled in where necessary, such as "soft mallets," "wood sticks," "two beaters."

14. *V.S.* (volta subito—It. "turn quickly") should be marked in large letters at the end of a page which requires a quick turn.

15. Brackets should be drawn to enclose rhythmic figures which cross bar lines or are otherwise not readily apparent, as in A and B below.

SUBSTITUTION OF PERCUSSION INSTRUMENTS

Occasions will arise in all but the most completely equipped bands and orchestras when it will be necessary to substitute an available instrument for one called for in the score but not procurable. It usually is better to improvise a substitution rather than leave the part out entirely. The following list of possible substitutions does not exhaust the potentialities, but may prove useful to the director as a guide in making necessary percussion instrument substitutions. It should be noted that, as a general rule, instruments of a similar pitch range and timbre are used as substitutes for the indicated instruments.

1. The bass drum can be used to play certain important timpani parts if these are of vital rhythmic or timbre importance. The bass drum cannot contribute the harmonic effects of the timpani, however. It is possible to use the large (16″ x 16″) tunable tom-toms from the dance drummer's set-up to substitute for the timpani in certain cases. With careful tuning these can be made to sound a fairly clear fundamental tone.

2. A triangle beater, spike, or snare drumstick striking the dome section of a suspended cymbal can be used to serve as a triangle, and has been used to substitute for even a bell note.

3. The best substitute for the tambourine is the snare drum played near the rim.

4. Castanet parts can be played by striking the top of a woodblock with the tips of snare drumsticks.

5. Woodblock notes can be obtained by using a snare drum rim shot of the cross stick variety (see Chapter 3, page 56). Very light woodblock notes can be imitated by playing on the rim of the snare drum.

6. Xylophone and marimba are interchangeable, provided the appropriate kinds of mallets are used. In making the xylophone serve as a marimba, use soft rubber or yarn-covered mallets. To play a xylophone part on the marimba, use medium or hard rubber mallets. As a general rule, play xylophone parts in the upper octaves of the marimba. Play marimba parts on the lower octaves of the xylophone.

7. Bells and vibraphone parts can be substituted for each other. Do not use the "vibra" mechanism when playing bell parts on the vibraphone. Transpose written bell notes up two octaves if played on the vibraphone. Make the opposite transposition if playing vibraphone notes on the bells.

8. Chime parts can be played on the bells or the vibraphone, doubling at the octave in the lowest possible range.

9. Here is an ingenious substitute for the tuned antique cymbals (crotales) called for in Debussy scores and other works. Remove the bell bars corresponding to the pitches of the antique cymbals

called for (e″ and b‴ in DeBussy's *L'Apès Midi d'un Faune*). Place these bars on a pair of heavy rubber bands stretched around a cigar box with its top removed. Use metal bell mallets on the bars, striking very lightly.

Figure A6. Bell bars can substitute for antique cymbals.

10. The triangle can be used to substitute for the bells, although this is not a satisfactory substitute if the passage is melodic in nature.
11. The snare drum, especially the field type with snares turned off, makes an excellent substitute for the tom-tom. The field drum with no snares may serve very satisfactorily as a tenor drum.
12. A large suspended cymbal struck with a timpani stick can be used to substitute for a tam-tam (gong).
13. The woodblock can be substituted for temple blocks. To obtain two tones from a single block, strike with the tip of the snare drumstick on top of the block for a light, high pitched tone, and with the shoulder of the stick on the edge for a deeper, more resonant tone.
14. Different size snare (with snares off), field, or tenor drums or any combination of these played with medium or hard timpani sticks can be substituted for a set of concert tom-toms. Modern scores, particularly band scores, call for these instruments frequently.

When all of the written parts cannot be covered by the number of percussionists available, it becomes necessary to insure that the most important instruments will be heard and only the least essential will be left out. Every case demands the attention of the director, and no two cases will be exactly alike. The

two general rules that may guide the director or percussionist are: 1) leave out those notes or passages which contribute least to the total musical effect, and 2) leave out those passages which are played by another percussion instrument in the same general pitch-timbre range. As an illustration of the latter rule, if timpani and bass drum play a similar rhythm pattern the bass drummer can be spared to play a triangle part not covered by another player. Another illustration: when gong and cymbal notes coincide, and the player cannot reach both instruments at once, leaving out the cymbal notes would probably be best, since the gong is more powerful and would tend to dominate the sound anyhow.

STAGE DEPORTMENT FOR THE PERCUSSION SECTION

The watchwords for the percussion section in concert are: 1) no unnecessary movement and 2) no unnecessary sound.

The first step to unobtrusive and efficient concert performance is to arrange the instruments, stands, music, trap tables, sticks, beaters, etc., in their most convenient location before the first downbeat. Each player should be responsible for the items of equipment he is to use during the concert, and the section head should oversee the group's preparations. Due to the complicated percussion set-up required by many contemporary compositions, ample time between numbers must be allowed. It is always wise for the conductor to make a visual check with the percussion section leader prior to giving his downbeat to make sure the section is prepared.

It is presumed that the parts have been definitely assigned and marked for the individual players during rehearsals. There is no excuse for confusion over who is to play what at concert time. During rehearsal periods one further matter should be worked out, and that is the timing of standing for entrances after rests. Incidentally, rests should be counted silently, and with a minimum of lip movement. Cross-checking of the count among the players may be done by a prearranged signal, such as a nod of the head or a small movement of the hand at each rehearsal letter. Lip-reading, provided that it is done discreetly, is an additional check. Each percussionist should have a chair and should sit during long rests and tacet portions of the program. In moderate or slow tempos a rest of over 16 or so measures will allow the player ample time to be seated and rise again for the next entry. One simple rule for rising for an entrance would be to rise four measures in advance in slow or moderate tempos, eight measures in advance in allegro and presto passages.

Particular care should be taken to eliminate the distracting extra sounds from the percussion section which mar so many performances. Dropped snare drumsticks can be prevented by a concert rest position which uses *both* hands, one at either end of the pair of sticks. See Figure A7. Some band directors

prefer a more military rest position in which the pair of sticks is tucked under the right arm with the ends held from underneath by the right hand. See Figure A8.

Do not allow the triangle beater to touch the triangle while getting into playing position, or let the triangle dangle where it will strike a stand, drum or timpani handle.

The tambourine is a treacherous instrument to prepare for playing and to put down after playing. The tambourine must be moved very slowly and carefully in order to keep the jingles from sounding.

A great aid to quiet functioning in the percussion section is a felt or baize-covered trap table. The type of folding tray stand used by bus boys is an excellent and portable base for a trap table. Cymbals, as well as the small traps, sticks and beaters should be placed on this table when not actually in use. Commercial trap tables are available, also.

Figure A7. Concert rest position.

Figure A9. Trap table.

Figure A8. Military concert rest position.

Snares should always be turned off at the conclusion of a snare drum passage preceding a long rest. This practice must be rigidly adhered to, as the buzzing of the snares during quiet passages is very annoying to the other musicians and to the audience. The snare drummer must also develop the habit of turning the snares back on just prior to entry—it is embarrassing to start a snare drum passage with a tom-tom tone.

Percussion students should be trained to arrive early in order to arrange their instruments and to tune them properly before the rehearsal or concert hour. The snare drumheads should be set, snare tension adjusted, bass drumhead loosened to its proper playing tension, and the timpani set for the tunings required in the first piece on the program. Of course the timpanist must recheck these tunings just prior to the first downbeat and, in fact, constantly if the atmospheric conditions are at all changeable. All the instruments should be tested prior to the playing period, and a thorough check made to see that all music, instruments, sticks, beaters, etc. are in order, and that music stands are placed so as to allow good sightlines to the conductor.

Snare drummers should try to avoid testing drumhead and snare tension during a performance. If it becomes necessary to make adjustments, test during a tutti passage where the sound will not be noticed.

The timpanist has a special problem in timing his tuning changes so that they will not be audible to the audience. He should use the finger flick and not the sticks to test intonation. If possible, he should locate the harmony or single tone to which he is tuning in a preceding passage. For instance, he may get his cue from a tuba note F# four measures ahead of his own entrance on an F#, and test his tuning quietly as the tuba sounds his note.

TWENTY MOST COMMON FAULTS OF SCHOOL PERCUSSION SECTIONS

1. Poor handholds, poor wrist action.
2. Snare drums set too low.
3. Snare drums not set on stands correctly.
4. Music stands too low for drums, timpani—too high for mallet-played instruments.
5. Not watching conductor closely enough, with resultant rushing or dragging.
6. Snare drumheads too loose.
7. Bass drumheads too tight.
8. Excessive noise, talking, fooling.
9. "Scurrying," which is distracting to audience.
10. Uneven tension on timpani, bass drum and snare drumheads.
11. Poor choice of sticks, beaters or mallets for the purpose at hand, i.e., snare drumsticks too light, timpani sticks too fluffy, triangle beaters too heavy, bell mallets too soft, etc.
12. Double stroke roll on timpani.
13. Hands through loops of cymbal straps.
14. Triangle left on stand while being played.
15. Snare drum snares vibrating sympathetically.
16. Failure to damp properly and at the right time (timpani, bass drum, cymbals, triangle, bells, chimes).
17. Failure to make the most of dynamic contrasts.
18. Careless counting.
19. Failure to listen to total ensemble sound.
20. "Faking."

Annotated Bibliography

PERCUSSION INSTRUMENT TEACHING AND REFERENCE MATERIALS

I. Snare Drum

COLLINS, MYRON D. *The Snare Drum at School.* Johnson-Hoffman, San Diego. Set of 10 booklets.

A course in snare drumming which has been designed for the school percussion class, particularly for those teachers with little or no background in percussion playing. Treats single strokes, rolls, flam, dotted notes, triplets, 6/8 time, expression marks and accents, abbreviations, ruffs, with an introduction to the rudiments. All counting and stickwork patterns written in for each exercise.

FENNELL, FREDERICK. *The Drummer's Heritage*, Carl Fischer Inc., New York.

A collection of old popular airs and official U.S. Army music for fifes and drums combined with similar pieces for field trumpets, cymbals and drums. An excellent source for the student of rudimental snare drumming. All of the music in this volume is recorded on Mercury MG 50111 *The Spirit of '76* and MG 50112 *Ruffles and Flourishes.*

GARDNER, CARL E. *Progressive Studies for the Snare Drum.* Carl Fischer, New York, 4 Vols., plus teacher's handbook.

Somewhat dated, but basically good full page studies for the snare drum student. Much explanatory material. Useful as supplementary reading material for the intermediate and advanced drummer.

GOLDENBERG, MORRIS. *Modern School for the Snare Drum with a Guide Book for the Artist Percussionist.* Chappell and Co., New York.

Probably the outstanding book in its field, this book treats snare drumming from a practical per-

formance standpoint rather than a rudimental one. Graded study material, including numerous duets, runs from easy to very difficult. In addition to the snare drum, excerpts and studies cover the bass drum, cymbals, numerous small percussion instruments and the Latin-American rhythm instruments. Percussion scores for 16 pieces from the standard orchestra literature are included, with notes on practical performance practices for each. Other features are the complete score of Varèse's *Ionisation* and a glossary of percussion terms in three languages.

HARRIS, ERNEST E. *The Solo Drummer.* G. Ricordi and Co., New York.

An album of original music for the snare drum. Solos, duets, trios and quartets, some with piano accompaniment. Contains several marching cadences, and themes upon which to base original compositions for the drum. Medium-to-difficult grade.

MCMILLAN, THOMAS. *20th Century Orchestral Snare Drum Studies.* Creative Music, Glenview, Ill.

An excellent collection of representative snare drum rhythm patterns from contemporary orchestral literature. Examples of the rhythms of such composers as Bartok, Chavez, Copland, and Stravinsky, only to mention a few, are presented. A great opportunity for the advanced drummer to study such devices as asymmetrical meters, asymmetrical divisions, shifted accents, changing meters, superimposed rhythms, etc.

OSTLING, ACTON E. *Three R's for Snare Drum—Reading, Rhythms, Rudiments.* Belwin, Inc., New York. Books *One* and *Two*.

A well-planned foundation course adapted for either individual or class instruction of the snare drum. Emphasis is on development of the practical technical and reading techniques most frequently used in the performance of elementary and intermediate school music. Each lesson contains one new element with illustrative studies, and one or two excerpts from standard literature which contain the new element.

PACE, RALPH C. *Variations of Drumming.* Drum Book Music, White Plains, N.Y.

Copious study material for the snare drum, emphasizing reading. Later bass drum and cymbals added for coordination studies. Many meters used, with very difficult studies toward end of book. No pictures, minimum of text. Not for the beginner, but good foundation for the preprofessional drummer.

PODEMSKI, BENJAMIN. *Podemski's Standard Snare Drum Method.* Mills Music Inc., New York.

Although a method book, its chief value lies in the many and varied exercises and etudes for the snare drum. These make for good reading material. It also has a very short and incomplete section on the timpani.

PRICE, PAUL. *Beginning Snare Drum Method.* Morris, New York.

A musical approach to the snare drum. Includes some 250 studies derived from the rudiments, many of which are in 8 measure tap step form. The treatment of the roll, and the fine photographic illustrations of playing positions, handholds, etc., make this a good book for either individual or class instruction. Developed by a college percussion instructor, and particularly adapted for use with mature students.

STONE, GEORGE L. *Stick Control for the Snare Drummer.* Geo. B. Stone and Son, Inc., Boston.

An advanced study book consisting of progressively arranged permutations of stickwork patterns of certain rhythmic figures. The value of such calisthenics lies in the attainment of good control over the sticks. The mind and hands are disciplined simultaneously. Very valuable supplemental study for the ambitious snare drum student.

STRAIGHT, ED. *The Straight System.* Books 1 and 2. Frank's Drum Shop, Chicago.

An old, but still much-used, method which emphasizes reading skills. Book 1 includes 50 odd page-length studies in 2/4 (some in C and 4/4) emphasizing quarter, eighth and sixteenth notes in varied combinations. Only the practical rudiments such as strokes, taps, flam, drag, and stroke rolls are used. Bass drum parts are included in some of the studies. Written to develop the technical and reading skills requisite for pit and vaudeville drumming. The explanatory text is replete with admonitions to "watch the leader," etc. The stick-

work is strictly right-lead. Book 2 is mostly 6/8 meter.

WILCOXON, CHARLEY. *The All-American Drummer.* Chas. Wilcoxon, Cleveland.

Contains 150 rudimental solos progressively arranged with all stick indications and rudiments carefully labeled. Exploits full range of the 26 rudiments.

WILCOXON, CHARLEY. *Modern Rudimental Swing Solos for the Advanced Drummer.* Chas. Wilcoxon, Cleveland.

Presents, in solo form, some of the standard rudiments varied through changes of accents, etc. Thirty-two solos, one or two pages each. Progressively arranged from medium difficult to very difficult. More rudimental than "swing." Not for double drums.

YODER, PAUL. *Rubank Elementary Method—Drum.* Rubank, Chicago.

One of the volumes in the Rubank Elementary Education Library Series. Exercises for the beginning snare drum student. Contains a few pages of studies for the bass drum, cymbals and small instruments. The 26 rudiments are included for reference. Stickwork indications are not those generally used in playing the typical snare drum rhythm figures.

II. Mallets

BARNETT, WALLACE. *The Mallet Percussions and How To Use Them.* J. C. Deagan, Inc., Chicago.

This guide contains brief but pertinent resumes of each of the mallet instruments. This pamphlet could be an aid when purchasing keyboard percussion. The publication also contains a compilation of performance material, from all publishers, in which the mallet instruments are used.

BURTON, GARY. *Four Mallet Studies.* Creative Music, Glenview, Ill.

A study of the problems involved in playing with four mallets. Although much of the technique discussed is applicable to all mallet instruments, the book concerns itself with the "vibes." It deals with holding the mallets (with good pictures), hand and mallet independence, and voicing techniques. All areas contain a considerable amount of exercises and examples. This is a good book for the aspiring jazz vibe player.

BURTON, GARY. *Solo.* Creative Music, Glenview, Ill.

A collection of six unaccompanied solos for the vibraphone. Sticking, use of the damper, and chordal structures are well marked. These solos range from medium difficult to very difficult.

DEVENS, GEORGE. *Lesson Plan for Mallet Instruments,* a Musical Approach to Technique for Vibes, Marimba, Xylophone. Henry Adler, Inc., New York.

Guide to ideas on technique studies, to be extended and transposed to all keys. Intended as a foundation book for the mallet player preparing for jazz or studio field. Stress is on technique building, not reading.

GOLDENBERG, MORRIS. *Modern School for the Xylophone, Marimba, Vibraphone.* Chappell and Co., New York.

A complete method for the mallet-played instruments. Scale and chordal studies in all keys, with related melodic materials comprise the first half of the book. These are graded from easy to very difficult. The latter half of the book contains excerpts from standard orchestral literature. A must for all serious students of the mallet instruments.

GORNSTON, DAVID. *Foundation Studies for Vibes, Xylophone or Marimba.* David Gornston, New York.

Contains graded original major and minor scale and chord studies, plus 15 pages of studies adapted from Klose and other sources. These studies run a full page each and are excellent for the building of a fine mallet technique.

GREEN, GEORGE HAMILTON. *New Elementary Studies for Xylophone and Marimba.* Leedy and Ludwig, Elkhart, Indiana.

Mallet studies for the beginner, including all of the major and minor scales. Exercises are adequate from a technical standpoint. No excerpts or pieces.

KRAUS, PHIL, ed. ALLAN, DOUG. *Modern Mallet Method,* Vol. I Elem., Vol. II Inter., Henry Adler, Inc., New York.

Progressively arranged technique exercises, mostly in sequence form. Little melodic material. Theory, especially harmony, well treated. Good supplementary material for the ambitious student preparing for jazz and studio work.

PETERSON, HOWARD M. *Rubank Elementary Method—Marimba or Xylophone,* Rubank, Inc., Chicago.

A foundation course for individual or like-instrument class instruction. Contains basic technical studies, mostly easy, and many familiar tunes. Some of the melodies are arranged as duets and trios. Good beginning book for young students.

SCHAEFER, FLORENCE. *Xylophone and Marimba Method,* Vol. I. Henry Adler, Inc., New York.

Basic mallet instrument instruction for the very young beginner. Uses folk song materials, quizzes, tests, blank pages for notes, and similar teaching aids. Contains 174 short exercises. Adapted for private or class instruction.

STONE, GEORGE L. *Mallet Control for the Xylophone, Marimba, Vibe.* Geo. B. Stone and Son, Inc., Boston.

Supplemental sequential studies for the mallet-played instruments, to be memorized and transposed to other keys. Designed to build a sound and facile technique. Studies are made up of diatonic scale patterns, arpeggiated chords, and double stops.

III. Timpani

FIRTH, VIC. *The Solo Timpanist.* Carl Fischer, Inc., New York.

Designed for the advanced player, this is a fine collection of 26 etudes for solo timpani. Each of the etudes deals with problems related to some of the most difficult works in the classical and modern repertoire, problems such as complicated meter changes, technique on six timpani, piano-staccato playing in the low register, cross sticking, tuning, and melodic passages.

FRIESE, ALFRED, and LEPAK, ALEXANDER. *Timpani Method.* Henry Adler, Inc., New York.

A truly complete timpani method, including extensive modern repertoire. Recognizes *intonation* as the central problem in timpani playing and devotes many pages to tuning study. Presumes the use of pedal timpani. Some studies for 3 and 4 kettles. In four parts: Basic Theory, Technique and Facts, Intonation, and Repertoire. A must for all serious timpani students.

GOODMAN, SAUL. *Modern Method for Timpani.* Mills Music, Inc., New York.

A complete timpani method in four sections: 1) Fundamentals, 2) Exercises for the Development of Technique on 2 Drums, 3) 3 and 4 Drum Technique, including Pedal Tympani, 4) Repertoire. Careful and copious explanations accompany the musical studies. An excellently selected repertoire of 22 selections, plus 2 original solos. Author is timpanist of New York Philharmonic. A must for serious timpani students.

HARR, HASKELL W. *Method for Tympani.* M. M. Cole Pub. Co., Chicago.

An inexpensive beginning timpani method, satisfactory for young elementary students. Contains some of the author's rudimental snare drum solos adapted for the timpani.

LUDWIG, WM. F. *Ludwig Tympani Instructor.* Ludwig Drum Co., Chicago.

A beginning method book included with all new WFL timpani. Diagrams and illustrations show proper playing positions, handholds, etc. In addition to the tuning and technique studies, information is given on the care of the timpani heads, storage, etc.

SIETZ, J. FRED. *Sietz' Modern School of Tympani Playing*. Leedy Mfg. Co., Elkhart, Ind., (out of print).

A complete timpani method, containing historical information and many illustrations. Theory of music and lists of musical terms and foreign language percussion terms are included. Tuning and technical studies for two to five kettledrums comprise the first section of the book. Orchestral excerpts make up the bulk of the book (130 pages), including all of the Beethoven symphonies and excerpts from the principal Wagnerian operas.

IV. Comprehensive Percussion Methods

BARTLETT, HARRY R. *Percussion Ensemble Method for Teacher Education*. Wm. C. Brown Co., Dubuque, Iowa.

Designed as a semester course text for the college-level instrumental class. Aims to develop the basic skills of playing all the percussion instruments through ensemble studies and pieces. The snare drum is considered as the basic instrument. Includes studies and pieces for various combinations of snare drum, bass drum, cymbals, timpani, mallet-played instruments, the small percussion instruments, Latin-American instruments and the dance band drum set. Emphasis is on musical and practical performance techniques.

FIRTH, VIC. *Percussion Symposium*. Carl Fischer, Inc., New York.

A very fine manual defining and illustrating the complete percussion section. It covers the areas of tone production, sound projection, instrument range, selection of correct sticks, proper care of instruments, and interpreting percussion notation. Although not a method book in the general sense, this publication is a source of practical reference for all those interested in the art of percussion playing.

GARDNER, CARL E. *Gardner Modern Method for the Instruments of Percussion*. Carl Fischer, New York.

In three parts. Complete in one volume or separate. Part One: Drums, Cymbals, Accessories (120 pp.), Part Two: Bells, Xylophone, Vibraphone, Marimba, Chimes (105 pp.), Part Three: Timpani (95 pp.). A standard method book presenting a unified approach to all the standard instruments of the percussion family. Thorough and correct expository text, clear instructions in technical matters. Copious studies, with many drawn from the standard

literature. Many of the excerpts, however, are from works seldom played today. Originally copyrighted in 1919, the newly revised and enlarged edition dates from 1938.

V. Set Drumming

BURNS, ROY, and MALIN, LEWIS. *Practical Method of Developing Finger Control*. Henry Adler, Inc., New York.

Photos illustrate snare drumstick handholds used in modern jazz drumming. Stress is on the fulcrum (grip), finger control and bounce technique. Designed for pre-jazz training. Some reading material is included written for four-way hand and foot coordination at the drum set. Studies are in the form of short patterns.

CHAPIN, JIM. *Advanced Techniques for the Modern Drummer*. Jim Chapin, New York.

The exercises in this book are designed to aid the jazz and dance drummer in perfecting the independent hand and foot coordinations characteristic of modern drumming. Most of the studies consist of one or two lines of counterrhythms against the basic cymbal jazz beat and steady bass drum beat in "two" or "four." Snare drum technique and some experience at the drum set are prerequisites.

DAWSON, ALAN, and DeMICHEAL. *A Manual For The Modern Drummer*. Berklee Press Publications, Boston.

A three part book dealing with the fundamentals of set playing, dance-band drumming, and jazz drumming. Presents the basic beat patterns of all major dances and follows each with suggested variations and embellishments. Offers background material on various styles and name players.

LUDWIG, WM. F. JR. *Modern Jazz Drumming*. Ludwig Drum Co., Chicago.

Supersedes Bill Ludwig Jr.'s original book on dance drumming, called "Swing Drumming." Attempts the difficult task of conveying the skills of dance band and jazz drumming via the printed page. Its value is much enhanced by the 130 photos and diagrams which clarify the concepts presented. A good book for the drum student beginning work at the drum set.

MORELLO, JOE. *Rudimental Jazz*. Jomor Publications, Chicago.

This is a modern application of the "old" rudiments to the drum set. Many of NARD's 26 rudiments are discussed with extensive examples and exercises given utilizing these rudiments in jazz drumming. This is a good book for those brought up on the "rudimental system" and are now learning dance and jazz band drumming.

RALE, PHIL. *Latin-American Rhythms for the Drummer.* Remick Music Corp., New York.

Adaptations of rhythms of the Latin dance forms for the drummer working at the drum set. Some illustrations and adequate exercise material. Mambo and cha-cha-cha not included, as this book was published prior to their introduction into this country.

REED, TED. *Progressive Steps to Syncopation for the Modern Drummer.* Ted Reed, New York.

Study material for "double drums." Exercises vary in length, many full page solos. Syncopation, ties and accents are main problems stressed. No rolls or rudiments. A practical reading book for the ambitious student learning to work at the drum set.

RICH, BUDDY. *Modern Interpretation of Snare Drum Rudiments.* Henry Adler Inc., New York.

Ghost written by Henry Adler, this book attempts to adapt the standard rudiments to usable form for dance band and jazz playing. The entire first half of the book consists of the 26 rudiments in varied notations. Although the rhythms derived from the rudiments do not seem "modern" today, the book does contain a lot of good reading material for snare drum sight-reading.

STERNBERG, SIMON. *Modern Drum Studies.* Alfred Music Co., Inc., New York.

A practical study book for double drums. The first section of the book consists of 312 30-40 bar studies, mostly 4/4, progressing very gradually from easy to very difficult. All are scored for snare drum and bass drum. The idioms are not rudimental, but neither are they jazz. Mastery of these studies provides ample foundation for the reading at sight of typical show drum parts. Contains a section on Latin-American rhythm instruments, and concludes with a short section on timpani.

WILCOXON, CHARLEY. *Drum Method.* Chas. Wilcoxon, Cleveland.

An attempt to integrate the original 26 rudiments and "swing" rhythms with most studies and solos written for snare drum, cymbals, etc., and bass drum. Designed for the drum student beginning study at the drum set.

VI. Marching Band Percussion

CASAVANT, A. R. *The Antiphonal Drum Section.* Southern Music Company, San Antonio.

A collection of exercises which may be used in whole or part as drum cadences or as drum music to be played in conjunction with standard marching music. These exercises or cadences serve as an introduction to the various types of contrasting rhythms that may be used with the snare, tenor, bass drum, and cymbals.

PETERS, MITCHELL. *Drum Music To March By.* KSM Publishing Company, Dallas.

A collection of drum cadences with the first half of the book devoted to a wide selection of binary and ternary meter cadences with traditional style and instrumentation. The second part of the book presents cadences which are based on various styles of popular music such as "rock and roll."

SCHINSTINE, WM. and HOEY, FRED. *Drum Cadences for All Occasions.* Southern Music Co., San Antonio.

A booklet of march beats in a variety of styles, scored for snare drum, cymbals and bass drum. Based on 6 rudiments. A good source of beats for school marching groups.

VII. History of Percussion

FARMER, HENRY GEORGE. *Handel's Kettledrums and Other Papers On Military Music.* Hinrichsen Edition Ltd., London.

A historical survey of English military music with considerable emphasis on the percussion involved. Purely of historical interest.

HOWARD, JOSEPH. *Drums In The Americas.* Oak Publications, New York.

Dr. Howard, one of the country's leading authorities on drums, discusses in this book the heritage of the drum in the Americas from its communal use as an instrument of warning through its final evolution as a musical instrument. Very nicely illustrated.

WHITE, CHARLES. *Drums Through The Ages.* The Sterling Press, Los Angeles.

A very readable volume on the history and evolvement of percussion instruments around the world. Interesting as background material on percussion.

VIII. Orchestration of Percussion

KENNAN, KENT. *The Technique of Orchestration,* 2nd Ed. Prentice Hall, Inc., Englewood Cliffs, New Jersey.

Although only two chapters of this publication is devoted to percussion, it is worth consulting regarding any problems involved in writing for percussion. This edition was published in 1970 so is generally quite up to date.

Leach, Joel and Reed, Owen. *Scoring for Percussion.* Prentice-Hall, Inc., Englewood Cliffs, New Jersey.

This book provides a rather detailed analyses and description of the various percussion instruments along with a modern approach to understanding how to notate for these instruments. Areas included in the book are availability of the various percussion instruments, ranges and sizes of the instruments, transposition of the mallet instruments, ways of setting the instruments into vibration, various types of beaters available, standardized notation, and percussion as an integral part of the compositional scheme.

RECORDINGS OF SPECIAL INTEREST TO PERCUSSION PLAYERS AND TEACHERS

American Percussion Society—Price, Cond., Bartlett: Four Holidays for Three Percussionists; Colgrass: Three Brothers; Harrison: Canticle #3 for Percussion; McKenzie: Introduction and Allegro; Varèse: Ionisation—*Urania UX-106; stereo 1007.*

Boston Percussion Group—Chavez: Toccata; Farberman: Evolution—*Boston 207.*

Concert Arts Orchestra—Slatkin, cond., Milhaud: Concerto for Percussion and Small Orchestra—*Capitol P-8299.*

Eastman Symphonic Wind Ensemble—Fennell, cond., Ruffles and Flourishes—*Mercury 50112; stereo 90112.*

Eastman Symphonic Wind Ensemble—Fennell, cond., Spirit of '76—*Mercury 50111; stereo 90111.*

Eastman-Rochester Orchestra—Hanson, cond., McPhee: Tabuh-Tabuhan—*Mercury 50103.*

Elden Bailey (with A. and M. Ajemian)—Hovhaness: Suite for violin, piano and percussion—Columbia ML-5179.

Gotham Percussion Players—Chavez: Toccata—*Urania 7144.*

Ithaca Percussion Ensemble—Benson, cond., Percussion—*Golden Crest 4016.*

Izler Solomon and ens.—Villa-Lobos: Choros #7—*MGM 3155.*

Julliard Percussion Orchestra—Waldman, cond., Varèse: Integrales; Ionisation—*EMS 401.*

Kapp Sinfonietta—Stravinsky: L'Histoire du Soldat—*Kapp 6004; stereo S-6004.*

Los Angeles Contemporary Music Ensemble—Craft, cond., Antheil: Ballet Mechanique—*Urania UX-134; stereo 1034.*

Manhattan Percussion Ensemble—Price, cond., Chavez: Toccata; Hovhaness: October Mountain; LoPresti: Sketch—*Urania UX-134; stereo 1034.*

Manhattan Percussion Ensemble—Price, cond., Cage, Harrison: Concert for Percussion Orchestra—*Time 58000; stereo 8000.*

Minneapolis Symphony—Dorati, cond., Taylor, narrator—Britten: Young Person's Guide to the Orchestra—*Mercury 50055.*

New Sounds From Paris—Jean-Claude Casadesus and Jean-Pierre Drouet, percussionists; Boucourechliev: Archipel I—*Angel S-36655.*

New York Percussion Ensemble—Glick, cond., Bach: Toccata and Fugue in d, F: Fugues in g and C—*Audio Fidelity 1812.*

New York Percussion Group—Surinach, cond., Antheil: Ballet Mechanique—*Columbia ML-4956.*

New York Percussion Group—Surinach, cond., Glanville-Hicks: Piano and Percussion Sonata (Bussotti)—*Columbia ML-4990.*

New York Philharmonic—Bernstein, cond.; Bernstein: Symphony No. 3, Kaddish—Columbia KL6005.

Percussion Ensemble—Price, cond., Percussion Music—*Period 743; stereo S-743.*

Percussion Groups—Kraus, cond., Allan: Conflict; Colgrass: 3 Brothers; Kraus: Kriss-Kraus; McKenzie: Nonet and 3 Dances for Percussion; Wuorinen: Prelude and Fugue—*Golden Crest 4004.*

Robert Craft and Ens.—Boulez: Le Marteau sans Maître—*Columbia ML-5275.*

Saul Goodman—Mallets, Melody and Mayhem (collection)—*Columbia-1533; stereo 8333.*

Stuttgart Pro Musica—Bartok: Sonata for Two Pianos and Percussion—*Vox PL 9600.*

Vienna Choir and Ens.—Rossi, cond., Stravinsky: Les Noces—*Vanguard 452.*

Instructional—

Bongo Drum Instruction—Folkways 8320

Haskell W. Harr's LP Lesson Record with Drum Method #2—Slingerland Drum Co., Chicago, Ill.

Percussion Performance #1—Mervin Britton demonstrates tambourine, castanets and triangle—3 color filmstrips and study manual are included with LP record—Lyons Band Instrument Co., Chicago.

Shelly Mann Drum Folio No. One (music and record)—Music for Percussion, Inc., New York.

Spotlight on Percussion—Vox DL 180.

The Thirteen Essential Drum Rudiments—Ludwig Drum Co. record #1.

The Twenty-six Standard American Drum Rudiments —Ludwig Drum Co. record #2.

ADDITIONAL REFERENCES

BARTHOLOMEW, W. T. *Acoustics of Music*, New York: Prentice-Hall, Inc., 1942.

BARTLETT, HARRY R. *How to Play the Latin American Rhythm Instruments*, Berkeley: Wynn Music, 1958. (Pamphlet)

CULVER, CHARLES A. *Musical Acoustics*, Philadelphia: Blakiston, 1947.

Harvard Dictionary of Music, ed. Apel, Cambridge: Harvard Univ. Press, 1955.

READ, GARDNER L. *A Thesaurus of Orchestral Devices*, New York: Pitman, 1953.

SACHS, CURT. *The History of Musical Instruments*, New York: W. W. Norton, 1940.

—————. *Our Musical Heritage*, New York: Prentice-Hall, 1948.

SPINNEY, BRADLEY. *Encyclopedia of Percussion Instruments and Drumming*, Vol. I and II, Bradley Spinney, Kew Gardens, L.I., New York.

Glossary

GLOSSARY OF PERCUSSION TERMS

Including Some of the More Common French, German and Italian Equivalents.

(For names of percussion instruments, with their foreign equivalents, see table of percussion instruments Chapter 2.)

English	French	German	Italian
(with) brush, brushes, wirebrushes	brosse balai métallique	drahtburste	scovolo di fil di ferro
buzz roll (a snare drum roll so closed that individual sounds blend into a continuous tone)			
cadence (marching beat for drums, usually 8 measures long)			
change tuning (timpani)	changez	nach-stimmen	muta
choke (damp cymbal quickly)	étouffé	dämpfen	secco
clashed (pair of cymbals)	a l'ordinaire	becken gewöhnlich	a 2
closed (closely spaced individual strokes, taps and bounces—snare drum rudiments)			
collar (that portion of a drum or timpani head which extends from the flesh hoop to the edge of the shell)			
damp, dampen (stop vibration suddenly by contact with fingers or hands)	étouffé	dämpfen	secco
double, double stroke (successive *pairs* of stick alternations RRLL etc.)			

English	French	German	Italian
double drums (snare and bass drums played by the same player, through use of the bass drum foot pedal)			
double stops (two-note chords on the mallet-played instruments)			
double tension (drums with separate tension casings attached to the shell for each tuning rod. Heads tune independently)			
drum (generic term)	caisse, tambour	trommel	cassa, tamburo
hammering (patterns of alternated or successive R or L strokes — mallet-played instruments, timpani)			
handhold (manner of grasping the stick, beater or mallet)			
hand-to-hand (alternating the snare d r u m sticking patterns in playing the rudiments)			
hard sticks	baguettes dures	schwerer schlagel	bachette dure
idiophone (percussion instrument w h o s e tone is produced by the body of t h e instrument vibrating, through striking, shaking, scraping, or friction)			
mallet (heavy)	marteau	Holzhammer	maglio
membranophone (percussion instrument w h o s e tone is produced by one or two stretched membranes [h e a d s, skins] vibrating through being struck)			
motor off (vibraphone)	non vibrez		
muffle with cloth (timpani)	voilée, sourdine	Gedampft	coperto, coperti
near rim	au bord	am Rand	sul bordo
on the knee (tambourine)	avec le genou	auf dem Knie gestrichen	col ginocchio
on the shell (of the drum)	sur la cadre du tambour	auf dem Holzrand der Trommel	sulla cassa del tamburo
on the skin (head)	sur la peau	auf das Fell	sulla membrana
on the snares	sur les timbres	auf den Saiten	sulla corde

English	French	German	Italian
open (widely spaced i n d i v i d u a l strokes, taps and bounces—snare drum rudiments)			
pedal off (vibraphone)	sans pedal	ohne pedal	senza pedale
percussion (section)	batterie	schlagewerk	batteria
piatti (the pair of clashed cymbals)	cymbales á 2	becken	piatti
playing spot (point on the head, bar, tube or surface where the beater should strike for maximum resonance)			
press roll (a short snare drum roll made by pressing both sticks onto drumhead simultaneously)			
rim (play on rim of drum)			
rim shot (drumstick contacts head and rim simultaneously)			
roll (technique of sustaining t h e tone of a percussion instrument by rapid alternations (single strokes) or successions (double strokes) of the sticks, beaters or mallets.	roulée	wirbel	rullo
rubbed together (clashed cymbal roll)	agitees l'une contres l'autre	triller (zu 2)	trillo (à 2)
rudiments (prescribed sticking of traditional snare drum rhythm figures and techniques)		anfangsgründe	
shake (tambourine)	agite	schütteln	agitare, trillo
single, single stroke (alternated sticking RLRL etc.)			
single tension (drums whose heads tension by means of single tuning rods connected to b o t h counterhoops [rims])			
snare, snares (set of four to twenty wire, gut, or combination wire-gut cords which pass under the bottom head of the snare drum and rattle against it when the drum is struck)	cordes, timbres	saiten	corde
(with) sponge-headed sticks (timpani)	(avec) baguettes d'éponges	mit dem schwamnschlagel	bachelle di spugna

English	*French*	*German*	*Italian*
stick beat (note, or notes, played by striking the shoulders of the snare drumsticks together in mid-air)			
stick, beater, mallet	mailloche baguette	schlagel, Klopper	mazza, bachetta
sticking, stickwork (patterns of alternated or successive R or L strokes or taps—snare drum, timpani)			
strike	frappez	schlagen	colpo
street beat (marching cadence for drums, usually 8 measures long)			
stroke (action of fingers, hand and arm, and stick, beater or mallet used to produce sound of percussion instruments)			
take drumstick	prenez la mailloche	mit der Schlagel	colla mazza
tap (a light stroke initiated by wrist action only)			
tap step (marching cadence for drums, usually 8 measures long)			
(with) timpani sticks	(avec) baguettes de timbales	(mit) paukenschlagel	(con) bachette di timpani
Tog. (abbr. of *together*) (bass drum and cymbals to play from the same notes)			
traps (the numerous small noise-producing percussion instruments, as triangle, woodblock, etc.)			
with the fingers (light tambourine stroke)	avec les doigts	mit den fingern	col il dita
with the thumb (tambourine thumb trill)	avec le pouce	mit dem daumen	col pollice
without snares (muffled drum)	sans cordes	ohne Schnaurseite, gedämpft	senza cordes
(with) wood sticks	(avec) baguettes en bois	(mit) Holzschlagel	Col legno, bachetto

NOTES

NOTES

NOTES